ISBN #0-87788-747-0

Cover design by Ron Kadrmas

Cover illustration © 1990, Paul Turnbaugh

Library of Congress Cataloging-in-Publication Data

Morrison, Jan.
  A safe place : beyond sexual abuse / Jan Morrison.
    p. c.m.
  Includes bibliographical references.
  ISBN 0-87788-747-0
  1. Sexually abused children—United States—Psychology.
2. Sexually abused teenagers—United States—Psychology.
3. Adult child sexual abuse victims—Rehabilitation—United States. 4. Self-help techniques. I. Title.
HQ72.U53M77 1990
362.7'6—dc20   90-34630
                                                  CIP

---

99 98 97 96 95 94

10 9 8 7 6 5 4

*for every teen
who has ever suffered
the horrors of being abused*

Contents

Acknowledgments *vii*

Introduction *xi*

Getting Acquainted

1   Just the Facts   *3*

2   The Real, True, Inside You   *9*

3   Angie's Childhood   *13*

4   Angie Grows Up   *31*

5   A Bag Full of Garbage   *41*

Sorting through the Trash

6   Scared to Death   *49*

7   I'm So Confused!   *59*

8   I Feel So Guilty   *63*

9   Struggling with Shame   *71*

10   I Hate You!   *77*

11   Innocence Lost   *83*

12   Who Can I Trust?   *89*

Acting It Out

13   The Control Game   *95*

14   Sex without the Love   *101*

15   The Great Escape   *107*

16   Life at Home   *113*

17   Especially for Guys   *121*

Getting Together, Learning the Truth

18   Support Groups   *133*

19   The Awesome Truth about God   *137*

20   The Real Truth about Love   *153*

21   The Wonderful Truth about Sex   *165*

Moving Ahead

22   The End of the Story   *181*

Just for You   *189*

Tree of Rest, Inc.   *191*

Dear Parents   *197*

Endorsements   *201*

Acknowledgments

A heartfelt thanks to:

Gene Edwards, for allowing me to use his wonderful story on the very first time the very first lovers made love;

David Peters for permission to use the letter from the girl whose uncle abused her;

my board for allowing me to put things on hold while I wrote this book;

my sons, Troy and Darren, and my daughter-in-law, Kim for their acceptance of me and their support for what I'm doing;

Norm for his insight and prayer that brought to light the garbage I was still carrying, and his persistence in making me deal with it and write about it;

Charlotte, Beth, Janice, Elaine, and Larry & Karen for putting up with my erratic timetable and emotional outbursts;

all the special people across the country who have encouraged me and prayed for me and this book;

and of course, God, who arranged for all of these wonderful people to be in my life.

The stories in this book are true. Sherry, Megan, Jack, Tonya, and the others are *real* people who have experienced *real* abuse. But in order to protect their privacy, their stories are composites of the characteristics and situations of various abuse victims who have journeyed beyond abuse with the author. And, of course, their names have been changed.

I hope the experiences and emotions these friends share in this book will be a tremendous help and encouragement to you in your own journey.

Introduction

Since an "Introduction" is for introducing, here goes: My name is Jan. I'm tall and thin and blonde, and I think I'm a pretty nice person to know. But I haven't always felt that way. I am a sexual abuse victim. I have personally lived through the horror, experienced the feelings of hurt, and acted out the bitterness and hatred that followed my abuse. But I've also experienced deep healing.

In my work with sexually abused teens in high schools, I've spent hours growing great friendships with young people who have experienced deep pain. I've attended rape trials and sat alongside victims as they confronted their abusers. I've relived my own story in listening to theirs. But my work isn't all sadness and pain. I've watched teens as they journeyed out of shame, guilt, anger, and hatred and started to grow into all they were meant to be. I've shared their joy as they gained the freedom to accept themselves as worthy, valuable human beings and the freedom to accept intimacy, love, and sexuality as beautiful gifts.

■ The Journey

This book was written to encourage you to make a journey—a journey beyond sexual abuse to a safe place where you are free to become all you are intended to be. It won't be an easy journey, I'll admit. The going will get very rough sometimes; there will be high mountains to scale and deep valleys to climb out of.

If your abuse has ended, you may be thinking, "Why should I go through all that struggle? It's over now. I'll just go on with my life from here." But that's a mistake too many of us make.

All of us sexual abuse victims need to understand that if we don't deal with the effects of our abuse, the ugly secret will definitely rear its nasty head and steal yet more of our lives—when we fall in love for the first time, when we deal with authority figures on the job, when we marry and want to share all of ourselves for the rest of our lives, when our children reach the age we were when we were abused, when we find ourselves in situations with "good" people, and the list goes on.

The effects of sexual abuse will not just go away, *but they can be conquered.* As we uncover together the lies that sexual abuse creates, you'll grow to understand the truth about love and sexuality as they were created to be. The truth will set you free to conquer the effects of your abuse. The results are worth the effort because it's in this freedom that you'll discover something truly special—the real you!

Although the journey will be your own—we can't all travel the same path or use the same "transportation" or move ahead at the same speed—you shouldn't try to travel alone. Friends your own age are great and ultimately important. It's good to be able to talk with them about the journey and your new discoveries. But your teen friends aren't equipped to help you chart the best route to your destination, no matter how much they want to help.

So ask a mature friend (if such a person is available to you)—a teacher, pastor, counselor, or the mom of a close friend—to help you get started. You will probably discover that you need the help of a professional trained in the area of sexual abuse for part of your trip.

One of the most important things you can do for yourself to make your journey easier and faster is to get into a support group with other teens who have been abused. The purpose of support groups is to help victims of abuse identify their emotions and understand their actions. Group members don't have to be "taught" to understand your situation and feelings. In a support group, you'll find friends who will accept you just as you are.

■ You're Unique!

Remember, you're unique. You're going to travel in your own way, along your own path, through your own pitfalls and high points, and at your own pace. But we're all aiming at the same destination: a truly safe place where trust and intimacy can grow, a safe place where we are free to build healthy relationships of all kinds, a safe place where true love can unite with healthy sexuality in a beautiful "celebration" of love—a celebration so precious you'll *want* to protect it until you can share it within the committed and secure relationship of marriage with the one person you've chosen to share all the rest of your life with!

Hard to believe? I know it is. I know you feel like everything sexual has already been ruined for you. I felt like that, too. But that's not how I feel now. Now I'm not ashamed of who I am. Now I'm not afraid to trust. Now I can give and receive real love. I made the journey, and you can, too—I promise.

Jan

Getting Acquainted

1

Just the Facts

BEFORE WE JUMP INTO THE HURTS OF THE PAST AND the promises of the future, let's step back for just a minute and take a look at the larger picture of sexual abuse. Did you know that 1 in 3 girls and 1 in 4 boys are sexually abused by the time they are 18 years old? Let those numbers sink into your head for a minute. There are lots and lots of young people out there who have experienced abuse in some form or another. It also means that none of you can grow up without having sexual abuse touch your life in some way—either you will suffer abuse or someone you care about will experience abuse.

So, you see, sexual abuse affects all teens. That's why it's important for you to understand the facts and the lies about sexual abuse. What is sexual abuse? What causes it? What are the results of sexual abuse? How can you get help? How can you help a friend? That's what this book is all about.

The best place to start is with the background information—the facts. The terrible truth is that there are many types of sexual abuse—and we use lots of different terms and categories to talk about them.

■ Child Sexual Abuse

If you are in junior high or high school, you probably don't think of yourself as a "child." Well, I don't think of you as a child either. I know you're facing the pressures of responsibilities and decision-making that would scare any adult. I know that the carefree and comfortable days of trust and play seem long ago to you.

But the terminology about abuse includes you in the classification "child" until you reach the age of accountability that is stipulated by your state laws. Usually that's eighteen, so in sexual abuse jargon, you fit the category of "child sexual abuse."

The definition of "child sexual abuse" differs from state to state, too. We're defining it as "any contact or interaction between a child and an adult when the child is being used for the sexual stimulation of the perpetrator or another person." That means *any* contact or interaction, including fondling, oral sex, intercourse, and the exploitation of children or young people used in pornography.

■ The Perpetrator

The perpetrator is the person who initiates the sexual abuse. Right away you have a picture in your mind of who that person (or persons) was for you. Most of the time—90

4

percent—the perpetrator is a man, so in this book when we talk about a perpetrator we'll use "he" and "him."

To make some sweeping generalizations, there are two general types of perpetrators. One type experiences the child victim as an adult. The other type of perpetrator experiences himself as a child. I know that's a confusing distinction, so let's take a closer look.

The first type of abuser would relate sexually to an adult if he could, but he's having trouble being a mature adult and maintaining healthy adult relationships. So he uses his child victim as an adult-replacement, imagining that the child is an adult.

This "adult" abuser usually didn't show sexual interest in younger children as he was growing up. Most of his dating relationships were with girls around his own age. Often he met a girl and got married just like all the other guys in his class or in his circle of friends. But when the responsibilities and demands of adulthood become hard for him to cope with, or when his adult relationships develop conflicts, he starts feeling powerless, impotent, inadequate. So he substitutes a girl child to replace the woman he no longer feels comfortable with. When he's with a child, he feels more in control because he has more experience and more knowledge and information than the victim has. Usually he abuses girls who are in his family.

Those who abuse within their own families (who see their child victim as an adult) are referred to as "intra-familial" or "incest" abusers. This category includes fathers, step-fathers, grandfathers, step-grandfathers, brothers, uncles, etc. Later in this book, we're going to read about Angie, whose first sexual abuser was her step-grandfather (whom she called "Papa"). Although they were not technically related by blood, they were in a family relationship. Papa's abuse of Angie was incest.

The second category of abusers are those who think of themselves more as children than as adults. This type of abuser tends to prey on boys more often than girls, and most of the time the victim is a child outside his own family.

Ever since this abuser was an early adolescent, he has only been sexually interested in children or people younger than himself. If he had any relationships with girls his own age, it was usually because the girl approached him or because he was unable to get out of a situation. Even if he is sexually involved with someone his own age, he still prefers involvement with children—and will continue to seek that involvement. If he marries, it's a marriage of convenience or an effort to cover up his acts of sexual abuse.

This type of abuser—sometimes called a "pedophile"—hunts for victims, getting a job or engaging in some outside activity that would bring him into contact with the age group of children he is interested in. When you hear an occasional story of a babysitter, teacher, or scout leader who abuses children, the perpetrator falls into this category.

■ The Victims

This is your category—and mine (and Heather's and Kim's and Sherry's and lots of others you haven't met yet, but you will soon).

Guys and girls of all ages can be abused. But since statistics show that one in every three girls are abused versus one in every four boys, I'll be referring to the victim most of the time as "she." Maybe your experience with abuse began so early that you can't even remember the first time. Maybe your abuser was a trusted friend or family member, or maybe your abuser was someone you didn't know well. Your abuse experience might have lasted a long time, even to the present, or maybe it was one time.

Victims are as different as people can be: some are rich, some are poor; some are movie-star gorgeous, some are plain; some are tall, some are short; some knew their abusers, some did not; some were tiny children, some were already teenagers; some were blonde, some were redheads, some were brunettes; some were fondled, some were photographed, some were raped. Each victim is unique.

But deep inside, all sexual abuse victims feel really lonely—like no one else feels and hurts the way we do. And that makes us feel terribly isolated from everybody else and a little weird. Do you feel like you're in it alone? Even though it's hard for you to believe right now, remember that there are many, many other teens out there who are feeling some of the same emotions and experiencing some of the same things you are. You'll be better able to accept that truth as you meet some of those teens in this book.

2

The Real, True, Inside You

ARE YOU FAT? SKINNY? SHORT OR TALL? ARE YOU QUIET and shy, or noisy and outgoing? Are you happy? Sad? Angry? Lonely? Are you good at anything, or do you feel good-for-nothing? Are you any or all of these things—sometimes?

Do you ever wake up wanting to sing? Do you ever cry hot tears into your pillow? Do you love to play? Do you thrive on work? Do you love? Hate? Do you do any or all of these things—sometimes?

Who are you? So much depends on what you've experienced, on how you see yourself. How do you find out about the real, true, inside *you*? How do you find out about the *you* you were meant to be?

■ Who You Are Inside

The real, true, inside *me* got so awfully lost and confused by the events of my childhood and early adult life that I spent years and years believing the lies my abuse told me about who I was. I wish I'd started discovering who I was really meant to be sooner. I wish I'd started when I was a teen.

If you're opening up this book because the hurts of your past or the hurts of the present are telling you lies about who and what you are, then these pages could mean starting on the path of discovering the real, true, inside you.

Don't be afraid of what you'll find inside yourself, no matter how bad or unworthy you might feel right now. I've worked with hundreds of teenagers over the last four years, and I haven't yet found one I didn't love. Every one of them is good, valuable, and worthy, and I'm proud to have them as my friends.

■ Friends

In this book you're going to meet a lot of my friends. If you've known the pain of abuse, you may react in many ways to the victims who share their lives in this book. Perhaps your heart will reach out in sympathy and support because you know their pain—firsthand—and you're ready to be friends. Or perhaps your heart will constrict with fresh waves of fear and anger because you know their pain, and you don't want to remember.

None of the friends in this book is just like you. None of their experiences of sexual abuse will exactly match your own. But you may be surprised to discover that some of them have felt very much like you have felt. You may be amazed to find that you are both different and the same.

And that's what makes friends so special. Knowing others helps us know ourselves. When we see ourselves as like or unlike these friends, it helps us put a finger on who we are. We hear our hurts expressed in words we couldn't find ourselves, or we watch tears come to other eyes when we run out of tears for ourselves.

The friends in this book, beginning with Angie, are here for you. As they share their stories, it may take great courage for you to step into their shoes. (It often takes great courage just to keep walking in your own.) It may hurt to hear their stories. But as you read about their abuse experiences, you'll see how the lies their abuse taught them caused them to behave in ways that are every bit as "bad" as you feel you are. You'll understand how they came to feel as "unworthy" as you feel. As you see them come to recognize the truth about themselves, you'll be able, maybe for the first time ever, to feel hope for yourself. You'll be able to believe the truth: if they can do it, so can you.

Right now I want to introduce you to Angie, whose story will run over the next few pages.

3

Angie's Childhood

ANGIE'S STORY IS NOT PRETTY. IF YOU WERE ABUSED emotionally, physically, or sexually as a child, Angie's story may be especially difficult for you to read. But her story is here to help you know her—as a friend. In the chapters that follow, we'll talk about Angie's emotions and actions after abuse, and we'll talk about yours, too. Angie's story starts with her earliest memory.

> The crawl space under Grandma's house wasn't high enough for the three-year-old to stand up. She crouched, holding herself tightly, tiny face pressed against skinny knees, as if she could squeeze herself smaller and smaller until she disappeared. She knew that spiders and bugs and worms lived in that crawl space: Uncle John had told her so, and

she had seen the webs when he opened the door and threw her inside. She tried not to cry or even breathe, fearful that the creatures would find her, but uncontrollable sobs shook her despite her best efforts.

When the first of the crawling things started up her leg, she gave up all hopes for silence and invisibility. "Get off!" she screamed. "Out! I want out—let me out!" She stamped her feet and waved her arms to shake the creatures loose. She ran into a web and felt the sticky strands against her face. There were spiders in her hair! "Let me out!" she screamed. "Somebody! Please let me out!"

At last, exhausted, she fell beside the door, whimpering "please." But she knew that no one would make Uncle John let her out. Soon she stopped begging, and only the sounds of her weeping came from her dark dungeon.

* * *

When Angie was four, Lady was her best friend. It didn't matter that Angie was a girl and Lady was a dog; they were best friends, and they loved each other.

Angie and Lady had been playing together one day when Angie's father stormed out of the house and grabbed the dog by the collar. "You've ruined this dog. She won't hunt. I've got to break her!" He dragged Lady down the hill, through the field, and toward the river.

Angie knew that Daddy often took Lady down

14

by the river to hunt for birds, but today was different. She watched her father and her friend until they were out of sight, thinking, "How did I ruin Lady? I hug her and ride her and pet her and feed her. I didn't do anything bad to her."

Several hours later, she heard her father's shouts. "Angie! Get out here and see what you did to this dog!"

When she saw the nail-studded collar and the blood matting the fur on her best friend's neck, she cried, "But Daddy, I didn't do that! I didn't make Lady bleed!"

The dog tried to come to Angie, but her father jerked on the dog's collar. "Stay away from her!"

"Daddy, don't—the nails are sticking her! Don't cry, Lady!"

"I want this dog to win trophies. This is a champion hunting dog, not a toy for you to play with. If you want me to take the collar off, leave her alone!"

Angie sat on the porch steps, confused and crying. She didn't know how, but she knew she had been the cause of Lady's pain. She knew her friend had been hurt because they loved each other. The only way her child's mind could figure out to protect her friend was to do what her father had ordered—leave Lady alone.

✳   ✳   ✳

Mother said there was nothing to be afraid of, but five-year-old Angie was afraid anyway. She couldn't see in the dark closet, and it seemed that the walls were getting closer. Though she had begged Mother not to put her in there, Mother said she had to. At first she'd called desperately for Mother to let her out, but Mother didn't come. She didn't even answer.

She cried herself to sleep several times. When she was awake, she felt hot and sweaty, and her breath came in short gasps. She imagined herself mashed by the walls. The five-year-old became hysterical as she screamed for a mother who wouldn't save her.

Finally, she could only sob. No sounds would come from her throat, sore and exhausted from screaming.

* * *

Angie fidgeted restlessly. "Where did Daddy go?" she asked the pretty lady behind the desk. It seemed like a long time since her father had left her in this office, saying he would be "right back."

"He's in the courthouse, that big building across the street," the lady told her. "He'll come to get you in just a few minutes."

Angie wasn't sure she wanted to go to the courthouse. "Will Mother be there? I don't want to see her. She left me in the closet, and I couldn't get out. Daddy said I wouldn't ever have to go in the closet again."

"No, you don't have to go with your mother." The nice lady smiled at Angie. "The judge will just ask you some questions, and then you can go home with your daddy."

16

"Isn't Mother going with us?" Angie pressed.

"No, your mother won't be living with you anymore."Angie felt confused. She was glad she wasn't going to have to see her mother today, but she wasn't sure she wanted her mother to go away forever. Who would take care of her? Who would feed her?

When Angie and her father got in the car to go home, Angie realized that it was true after all—her mother wasn't going home with them. Angie wasn't sure if she was happy or sad.

* * *

It seemed to Angie that things got better when she went to live with Aunt Lee. Daddy worked out of town all week, but his weekends at home were fun. Once he brought her a bicycle and spent all Saturday afternoon teaching her to ride. Sometimes he took Angie to watch him play softball or down to the creek to wade.

During the week, Aunt Lee spent time with her and let her help in the garden and with the cleaning. Angie loved watering and planting. The earth smelled so good, and it was exciting to watch seedlings push up through the soil, grow tall, and blossom with leaves and vegetables. Angie liked helping in the house, too. She felt safe, needed, and special.

When Angie started to school, Aunt Lee even took her shopping for school clothes and supplies, explaining to Angie that at school they would teach Angie to speak correctly and conduct herself as a proper young lady.

Being a proper young lady is important to Aunt Lee, Angie decided. *I'll listen real hard to my teacher and be a good proper young lady.* Angie was determined to ensure the approval and acceptance of the aunt who made her feel so safe.

But one warm evening toward the end of her first year of school, Angie ran into the kitchen to show Daddy and Aunt Lee a jar of lightning bugs and found her father and aunt arguing. As Angie came in, the argument ended, and her aunt abruptly left the room without even looking at her. She went into her room and firmly closed the door behind her.

Angie's stomach started to churn even before her father spoke. Something was wrong.

"Your Aunt Lee doesn't want you in this house any more," Daddy said, walking past Angie. He wouldn't look at her either.

"But why?" Angie followed Daddy into her room.

"She just doesn't want you here any more. I can't take you with me, so you'll have to live with Granny."

"But what did I do? Daddy, tell her I'll be good." Tears stung her eyes. "I can be a proper young lady!" she pleaded.

But her father was slamming the drawers open and closed, putting her clothes into a box. The box seemed to appear from nowhere just so there would be no delay in sending her away.

* * *

Angie loved her grandmother's house. It had a big front porch with a swing and three rocking chairs. The smells were wonderful because Granny was always cooking something. Angie especially liked to watch Granny make kraut. She helped cut up the cabbage and carried it to the big old crock on the back porch, where Granny would add "secret ingredients" until the kraut was ready to go in jars in the pantry. Granny sang about Jesus while she cooked. Angie liked Granny's songs; they made her feel happy and light.

Under the willow tree by Granny's porch is my favorite place in the whole world, Angie thought. *It's my very own place. I can have tea parties with all my doll friends while Granny sits on the porch and makes pretty lace.*

Angie especially loved the lace. "This is called 'tatting,'" Granny explained the first time Angie saw her making lace. "My mother used to put it on all my Sunday dresses. When you get bigger, I'll teach you to make it and you can put it on your doll's dresses."

"Then I can stay? You'll let me stay?" the child asked the question, fearfully fingering the fragile lace so that she wouldn't tear it.

"Of course I'm going to let you stay!" The old woman pulled the child into her arms. "I love you!"

Angie's heart danced. A place to stay—a safe place at last!

So, even though she was nearly seven and was too big for such babying, Angie curled up into Granny's lap. As they rocked back and forth, back and forth, on that big front porch, Angie pulled out her dwindling supply of trust and opened her heart to receive the love and security that had evaded her. This time it would be different. This time it would be O.K. Granny had said she loved her. Granny had said she could stay.

✳ ✳ ✳

Angie was surprised when she saw that her daddy was home before the weekend. But the old familiar sick feeling swept over her as she entered the house and heard him talking to Aunt May.

"Thanks for taking Angie, May. The doctors don't have any idea how long Mom will be in the hospital. I guess having a kid in the house was too much for her."

What is wrong with Granny? Angie wondered. *What did I do?*

Her father saw her in the doorway. "There you are, Angie. Your granny had a heart attack. Aunt May is going to take care of you for a while."

Another move. Another house. Angie went with Aunt May; she had no choice and she didn't care. Angie knew now that there was no safe place for her, no staying, no love that lasted. Not for her. And Angie knew why. She wasn't sure what it was, but something was wrong with her. Somehow she hurt people she loved. She'd hurt Lady, and now she'd hurt Granny.

* * *

Aunt May was a temporary stop—Angie understood that. Daddy was looking for someone else to take care of her.

Then Daddy started bringing Nita around. Angie thought she was pretty. She and her daughter, Beth, who was two years younger than Angie, seemed nice enough. Since Daddy seemed anxious for everyone to get along, they all went places and did things together.

But when Daddy told her that he was going to marry Nita and they would become a new family, Angie didn't feel much of anything. For eight-year-old Angie it was just another move, another change.

Although Angie didn't mind the new arrangement, her new "Mamma" certainly did. One afternoon when the little girls had been forbidden to go swimming, Angie and Beth made secret plans to run away from home. But since they whispered under the bedroom window, Mamma heard every word.

Nita strode purposefully around the corner of the house, grabbed Angie by the arm, and began to lash her with a large switch. "Going to run away?" she demanded, her voice as cold as her eyes. "And take my daughter with you? This is all your idea! My Beth would never do anything like this if you hadn't talked her into it."

21

The switch reddened Angie's legs until they were welted. Angie tried to break free, but her step-mother was too strong. Beth sat quietly against the wall of the house until her mother had completed Angie's punishment. She didn't resist as her mother pulled her away, warning her never to pay attention to anything that bad girl said.

* * *

Perhaps Angie could have lived forever with her step-mother's anger and severe punishment if it hadn't been for her daddy's response to the tension between his wife and his child.

Once when Mamma sent her to the store for pickles, Angie came home with her favorite dill pickles. She hadn't even thought about her step-mother wanting any other kind. But she had. Daddy walked in while Angie's "spanking" was being administered.

"What's going on here?" he asked.

"I sent this willful child to the store, and she came back with these!" Nita gestured disdainfully toward the jar of dill pickles.

"But she didn't say what kind she wanted!" Angie implored her father for support.

"Did you say sweet pickles?" Daddy asked Nita.

"She knew they were for hamburgers—we always eat sweet pickles with hamburgers. She did it just to spite me. She's got to be taught a lesson!"

Angie was sure Daddy would explain that it had simply been a mistake, but he just looked from the angry woman to the crying child, turned his back, and disappeared into the bedroom.

Angie knew then that her step-mother was in charge.

* * *

No matter how she felt about her new mother, Angie loved "Papa," her new step-grandfather. He smelled funny, didn't shave, and didn't talk much, but he always seemed glad to see her. Angie thought he was the nicest man in the world. Starved for the attention, she grew attached to the old man.

One extra-special day, Angie was going to be allowed to camp out all by herself up on the hill behind Papa's house. Because she was nine years old, she was big enough to use her uncles' old Boy Scout tent. She put food in the backpack just like a real explorer, and she wasn't a bit afraid to turn out the lantern and find the north star before drifting off to sleep.

She woke up to find something touching her leg. Startled, she jumped instinctively. "It's me." Angie was glad to hear Papa's voice.

But her relief didn't last long. Papa was touching her in places that made her uncomfortable. She started to pull away.

"Be still," Papa commanded. And she was still.

Then Papa took her hand and made her touch him. When she tried to pull her hand away, he said, "If you love me, you'll do this for me." His voice sounded strange, and Angie was afraid. She knew what was happening was wrong, but she did what he told her to do. She didn't want Papa to go away like Mother and Aunt Lee and Granny.

He was hurting her so bad she couldn't stop crying even when he told her to stop. After a while he stopped hurting her, but not before the old familiar terror swept over her: the terror of not being able to understand what was happening, the fear of whether or not she would die, the confusion about what she had done to make this happen, the pain that once again someone she had trusted had hurt her. The tent and the crawl space and the locked closet merged in her mind. *No one will ever help me,* she understood in a flash.

Papa left the tent without saying anything to Angie. She lay awake for most of the night, her hot tears a soft whimper among the other night sounds. But like always she finally ran out of tears. She was completely empty.

✳   ✳   ✳

"How long after someone does that to you can you have a baby?" Angie demanded to know. The three eleven-year-old girls stopped snickering for a moment and stared at her. Angie repeated the question, but none of the girls seemed to know.

Until that moment, Angie had been happy to visit her aunt during summer vacation. She was away from Mamma, and she got to play with girls her own age. Suddenly she felt sick.

"Call my Aunt Katherine—please!" she begged them.

Aunt Katherine was concerned, and she commented on how pale Angie was. "I'll be all right if I can just lie down for a while," Angie told her. But Angie wasn't at all sure she would be all right ever again. The girls had been talking about how women got pregnant. She knew that Papa had done that to her. She lay on the bed the rest of the day, her stomach knotted tight with fear. *Am I going to have a baby? What will Daddy and Mamma do when they find out?* She imagined their angry reactions. Later, when it was dark, she buried her face in the pillow to hide the sound of her sobs and cried herself to sleep.

Aunt Katherine thought Angie must be homesick. The next morning, she asked cheerfully, "How would you like to get a permanent in your hair? Some pretty curls?"

Angie thought it was a good idea. It would give her time to decide which was worst: telling about Papa now, or waiting until she was pregnant to explain what had happened. *Either way they'll be angry,* she thought. *How much worse can things get—even if I tell? Will they even believe me?*

But Aunt Katherine had noticed the tears of hopelessness in Angie's eyes.

"Come on, Angie. Tell me what's wrong. Do you want to go home?"

Angie couldn't speak. She shook her head. She could see that Aunt Katherine was concerned and confused.

"What is it, Angie?" The older woman knelt down in front of the child and looked into her face. "You can tell me what it is. Whatever it is, it can be fixed."

"No it can't. Not this. It's really bad. Mamma and Daddy are going to be so angry. Everybody's going to be so angry with me." Angie's voice cracked and the tears ran down her cheeks.

"I won't be angry with you, Angie."

"Yes, you will. Everybody will be. I did something really bad, and now I'm afraid I'm going to have a baby." Sobs wracked her body. "The girls told me what a man does to a woman to get her pregnant, and Papa did that to me."

Angie didn't look up. She didn't need to. She could feel her aunt recoiling as the information sank in. Finally, Aunt Katherine asked some questions.

"Angie," explained Aunt Katherine somewhat clinically, "women don't get pregnant every time. You aren't going to have a baby." She sat down at the table. "I'm going to call your dad at work."

"No! Please don't—don't tell Daddy!" Despite Angie's begging, her aunt made the call.

For a while they sat in silence in the kitchen, waiting for Angie's father. Then her aunt said, "What happened wasn't your fault, Angie." But the words were empty to Angie; she was sure her aunt didn't believe them either.

Her father arrived and disappeared into the bedroom with Aunt Katherine to talk. When they came out, Angie searched his face for the expected anger and didn't find it. His voice sounded sorry when he spoke to her.

"Don't worry. Nothing like this will ever happen to you again."

He left. Angie hadn't moved from her stiff kitchen chair. She wasn't surprised that Aunt Katherine and Daddy hadn't reached out to hold her. Who'd want to hold such a bad girl?

* * *

Angie had been home less than a day when she and her step-mother had their first argument. She couldn't remember how it started, but she'd never forget how it ended.

"No wonder Daddy did what he did to you! Sitting on his lap, kissing him, hanging all over him. What did you expect?" Her words hung in the air like an indictment.

Angie didn't know how to answer. She didn't know what she'd expected. She knew she hadn't expected him to hurt her. She hadn't known anything about sex until that night. And she still couldn't see any connection between loving Papa and what he had done to her. But Mamma was right. She did sit on Papa's lap and kiss him and hug him—so maybe it was her fault.

"You're evil!" her step-mother hissed at her. "You have bad blood in you, just like your mother! You're going to grow up to be a whore! Everybody can tell! It's all your fault!"

The thought flickered across Angie's mind:

Maybe I am evil. I feel *evil when I remember that night.* But the feelings of shame were too much for the child to bear. Desperately she searched for a way to escape her pain. *Mamma's saying this because we don't get along. It's just a weapon for her to use against me,* Angie told herself, burying her pain under the increasing bitterness she felt toward her step-mother.

✳   ✳   ✳

Angie didn't remember much about the old couple who lived next door, but she would never forget their blond Cocker Spaniel puppy. One night when she was eleven, her parents went to visit a friend in the hospital in another town and left her with the neighbors. The lady went to work the next morning, but her husband got into bed with Angie.

As soon as she woke up and felt his hands on her, she knew what was going to happen. She started to cry.

"Please don't hurt me!" she begged. But he didn't say anything. He didn't stop either.

But Angie's tears did. Angie closed her mind and spirit. *I'm dead,* she told herself. *Dead people can't cry.*

The puppy on the floor beside the bed looked at her as if he were sad that she was dead. *Don't worry, puppy,* she told him in her mind. *Don't feel sad; it's not your fault!* She didn't have words to explain to the puppy with compassionate brown eyes that it was easier for her to be dead for awhile than to live through what was happening to her.

The old man finally left the room. It was safe for Angie to be alive again. She scooped up the puppy and held him close, wetting his soft fur with all the tears she couldn't cry while she was "dead."

Now she had to face the fact that her step-mother had been right: she did have bad blood in her. She was evil. She was going to grow up to be a whore. This old man could tell; everyone could tell.

But she didn't want to be evil! She wanted to be good like she was supposed to be. But she knew she wasn't.

She hadn't screamed or tried to make Papa stop. When he told her to be still, she was still. When he told her that if she loved him she would touch him the way he wanted her to, she did what he showed her to do. He hadn't really forced her to do anything. He just told her what to do, and she did it. She could have found some way to stop him, but she hadn't. She had just lain there and cried like a baby.

Maybe it really was all her fault. Maybe she had made Papa have sex with her. She hadn't made him stop, and she hadn't made the old neighbor stop. It must be true. She was everything her step-mother said, and everybody could tell.

She knew she couldn't walk out of that house and face all the people in her world. To know that anyone who looked at her would immediately know she was so evil was more than Angie could deal with. Panic-stricken, she searched for a way out. Finally she found it.

> When Angie left the house where the old man
> lived, she left behind the memory of everything
> that had happened to her that day. What was too
> horrible for her to bear, she simply forgot.

■ Who Can Blame Her?

Who can blame Angie for trying to forget the terrifying and
ugly circumstances of her childhood? Who can blame her
for feeling guilt and shame and confusion and despair, and
even for wishing to die?

Angie's childhood experiences destroyed the real, true,
inside Angie. Once there was a child inside who was ready
to love, to trust, to feel, to enjoy, to be good. But many, many
people and events pushed aside the truth and exchanged
it for a *lie:* that Angie was dirty, evil, unlovable, and not
worth keeping.

And the lie took root in Angie.

■ When You Were a Child . . .

Maybe right now you're ready to throw this book out the
window and into the dumpster. If you've already had more
than you can take, feel free to give yourself a break. You
can come back to this part of the book and read the rest of
Angie's story when you feel ready.

4

Angie Grows Up

ANGIE'S STORY ISN'T OVER YET. SHE GREW UP TRYING to push away the past. She succeeded in submerging her shame, bitterness, and despair, but they were still there. And the circumstance of her adult life continued to feed those destructive emotions.

> Angie trembled as she stood in the County Common Pleas Court. At one point she took the hand offered by the woman beside her—another victim of the same man. Though it had been more than a year since her attacker had held a knife to her throat and raped her in her north-side home, Angie told the judge, "There are some things you don't get over. It does things to you and those around you."
>
> The smile on Angie's face as she read the

31

newspaper article about her rapist's conviction was clearly sarcastic. Only the tears in her eyes betrayed her pain. It didn't help that her attacker had been sentenced to forty years in prison. Angie felt no satisfaction that justice had been served; instead she felt guilty. Her attacker's sentence was just one more thing to feel guilty about. Even with an early release, that man would be at least fifty years old before he got out of prison.

It never occurred to her that she had been living in a prison of her own ever since the night her attacker had lifted her from her bed by her hair, slammed her face into the wall, and raped her.

The retired couple who lived next door had called the police after she appeared at their door holding a knife she'd taken from her kitchen after her attacker left. A woman officer talked with her while a policeman went upstairs to take her sheets and the t-shirt she'd been wearing. A fingerprint crew searched the room for prints. Angie was taken to an emergency rape center in one of the large hospitals of the city. A doctor "collected evidence" and gave her medication so she wouldn't catch any diseases her attacker might have had. After the doctor gave her something to help her relax, the police detective took her home.

The police treated her kindly. They drove her to the station to look through pictures of sex offenders and drug addicts. When she couldn't identify her attacker, a police artist made a sketch from her description. The detective assigned to her case drove past her home several times each night and sounded his horn just so she would know they were looking after her. Never did any of the law enforcement personnel suggest that what had happened had in any way been her fault.

But they didn't have to. Angie knew. The morning following the rape, Angie woke up hating herself. She was still alive. If she'd been a good person, she would have made the attacker kill her. Her step-mother had been right all along—her predictions were true. She was a whore. "Papa" had known it; the old man from next door had known it. Even a drug addict burglarizing her house could tell just by seeing her asleep in bed. She should have worn a long gown, or pajamas. It was wrong to sleep in only a t-shirt.

Angie spent hours in the bathtub and shower. She scrubbed until her skin was raw, but still she felt dirty. She slept in long-sleeved pajamas despite the August heat.

Nights were the worst—it was dark, and she was alone with the memories and her fear. Sleep became her enemy. Only when she was exhausted would she take a knife from the kitchen and make herself climb the stairs to her bedroom. Every night she would lock her bedroom door and move all the furniture in the room in front of it. Having protected herself as well as she knew how, Angie would eventually slip into restless sleep.

But always, before many hours passed, she was awakened by the sounds of her own screams. Her heart pounded so that she felt it would tear right through her chest. Drenched in perspiration and shaking uncontrollably, she would grope for the knife she'd hidden under the mattress. Clutching it tightly in both hands, she'd sit in the middle of her bed, alone, terrified, and crying until the sun came up.

In many ways Angie tried to escape. She visited an out-of-state friend for several weeks, and she moved in with other friends to avoid being alone. She cut her hair short and stopped wearing make-up.

However, after a few months, Angie finally appeared to those around her to have settled into a normal existence. Her hair grew back to its old style, and she wore make-up again. She even accepted a date now and then. Angie seemed to have everything under control.

And she did. Angie controlled the course of conversations, events, and relationships as much as possible. Soon she'd perfected the art of control.

Her friends began to tease her about her ability to control people: "Angie, you could talk any guy on the face of this earth into giving you the shirt off his back!" And it was true.

Angie could get what she wanted and leave a man thinking the gift was his idea in the first place. Some even thanked her for taking their gifts! Someone bought her $400 suits. One man gave her money and signed for her to buy a sports car. Someone else gave her money to start a business.

Angie used people. She knew it, and she hated herself for it. It didn't occur to her that using people was a way of life she'd learned from the people who had used her. While Angie knew she was using people, she didn't realize how thoroughly she hated men. Somewhere along the line, subconsciously, she had set out to destroy the entire male population of the United States single-handedly.

At first she told herself she was just getting involved with the wrong men. She told herself that all she wanted was someone to love and take care of her. But the truth was that a whole string of men—good men—had offered to do just that. Angie had refused them all. She did not—and never would—love any of them. The truth was that she only wanted men to love her so that she could hurt them when she left.

When Angie realized what she was doing, she came to believe that she was as evil as her stepmother had told her she was. *Only a truly evil person could derive pleasure from watching others suffer,* she told herself.

It never occurred to Angie that she suffered too. Each time she entered a new relationship, she hated herself more. She seemed to stand back and watch herself manipulate her new victim into a dependent position where she had the power to break him. Then she did. Every time she ended a relationship, Angie vowed she would never do it again. But she did—again and again.

Two years after she was raped, Angie accepted a position with an international corporation and moved out of state. No one in the new city knew about her past. She had a clean slate. For the first time in years, she felt that she was in control.

Angie moved with a sense of eagerness and anticipation. Things would be different this time.

And things were different. The job was tailor-made for her. As a field representative she traveled a lot, and her clients didn't expect her to become their friend. Men asked her out, but it was easy for her to be evasive. Angie was in control; she began to feel safe. She almost began to feel good about herself.

Five months after Angie's move to the new job, she agreed to go out for the evening with a woman coworker. Several men had asked her to dance, but she had refused.

Early in the evening a good-looking man arrived with an attractive, well-dressed woman. They danced well together, Angie noticed. After a couple of sets, the man approached Angie and asked her to dance.

"No, thank you." She smiled politely and turned away.

"Why not?" asked the persistent man.

"I don't dance."

"I'll teach you."

"I don't care to learn." There was more than a touch of annoyance in her voice.

He smiled and walked away. Half an hour later he came back—with flowers.

"Listen, I'm sorry if I offended you. Peace offering." He held out the flowers. "I really would like to teach you to dance. Can't we start over again?"

Angie was really annoyed now. "Since we didn't start to begin with, I don't see how we can start

over. Why don't you give the flowers to the lady you
brought with you? I don't want to dance and, if I
did, it certainly wouldn't be with you!"

So he went. But moments later, his well-dressed
companion was standing in front of Angie's table.

"Excuse me, but I believe there's been a
misunderstanding," she began. "You seem to think
that Grant and I are dating. We've known each
other for ten years. His brother is married to my
sister. We both like to dance. He called and said he
felt like dancing, so I said sure. We are not involved—not at all. Please feel free to dance with
him—or talk with him, or anything else you want."

Angie was astonished. "I'm—I'm sorry," she
stammered.

The woman laughed. "Oh, that's all right. Grant
wanted you to know, but he didn't think you'd let
him finish a sentence if he came over again. He's
really quite a nice person once you get to know
him."

"I'm sure he is. I just thought—Well, tell him
I'm sorry."

"I'll tell him."

Angie wanted to sink right through the floor
when she saw Grant walking toward her again—
with the flowers still in hand.

"O.K., let's try this again." At least he was smiling. "You don't dance, and you don't want me to
teach you. But you do eat, I assume."

"Yes, I eat—and I'm sorry. I guess I jumped to a
wrong conclusion."

"Well, let's just call it a mistake on both our

parts and start all over. So, will you take these," he said, holding out the flowers again, "and go to dinner with me this weekend?"

Angie wasn't sure if it was because he had such a nice smile or because she'd given him such a tongue-lashing, but she agreed.

Several times during the week she thought of the upcoming date with doubt and fear. *But I'm strong enough now not to manipulate a relationship,* she assured herself.

But Angie was wrong. By the time the date was over, she knew she was the same old Angie, the same evil Angie who used people. All her attempts to create a new life and to establish control had not made her into the person she wanted to be. She couldn't live with herself anymore, so she picked up a knife and walked into her bedroom.

It didn't occur to her that she planned to end her life with a knife because, inside herself, she felt it should have been ended with her attacker's knife the night she was raped.

■ A Happy Ending

Angie's story doesn't end there. She didn't die that night. But when Angie said, "There are some things you don't get over," she was right. But she has learned that you *can* get through and beyond the things you don't get over. And that's what this book is about: getting through and beyond the far-reaching effects of abuse.

■ Out of Darkness

Maybe reading about Angie's life has been especially difficult for you. Maybe you were raped. Maybe you have felt the anguish of nightmares or of fear that keeps you from sleeping. Maybe you remember the confusion of loving the person who abused you.

Angie's story is a story of darkness, but there is light at the end. Things get better—much better! I know. You see, the stories you have just read about Angie are actually about *me*.

As a child I was sexually abused by my step-grandfather and my neighbor. As an adult I was raped by a drug addict.

I've felt the shame and fear and anger you feel. I understand the confusion you encounter in your relationships. I've experienced the despair of believing it will never get better.

But now I know things *can* get better. That's why I wrote this book: to help you believe they can get better *for you*. Like I said before, it won't be easy; getting better doesn't just happen. First you have to learn the truth about abuse. Then you have to work to throw out the lies you learned and replace them with the truth. Learning the truth and replacing the lies are all part of your journey. As you travel, you'll begin to see that things are getting better for you—just like they got better for me and for hundreds of others like me . . . and like you. You'll meet some of these teens as you read this book and others as you make your own journey.

5

A Bag Full of Garbage

AS WE BEGIN TO LOOK AT THE RESULTS OF SEXUAL abuse, it's important that you understand that your feelings, no matter what they may be, are genuine and reasonable. Maybe your experience doesn't seem as "bad" or it hasn't lasted as long as someone else's.

Did your perpetrator hurt you only once? Were you forced to fondle but not to have intercourse? Were you abused over a long period of time? Were you molested by a stranger or by a trusted family member or friend?

No matter what happened to you, you need to understand that you will have emotional "garbage" left over from that episode in your life.

After I spoke in Joanie's church, I received this letter from her. She identifies many of the feelings that abuse victims battle, and she voices many of our thoughts.

Jan,

I know you're trying to help people. This is what I remember. Maybe it'll help you help me or help someone else. This is how I felt:

• This is going to go on forever, and I can't take it anymore.

• Lord, please make him stop. Why don't you make him stop? How can you let this happen to me?

• I can't tell on my own father. They'll send him away and ruin his life. It will humiliate and break up my family.

• What if I get pregnant? What will I do?

• If I tell, he'll kill me. If I don't, then it's my fault that it's going on.

• When I get married someday, things will never be right sexually. I don't know if I could ever love a man in that way. How could my husband ever forget that I let this happen to me, that I wouldn't stop my dad?

• I wanted to be pure, and now I never will be.

• Will it be worse the next time?

• Lord, don't let him hurt my little sister. Don't let him do this to her.

• Nobody will believe me anyway. They all look up to him. If I tell I'll be making a fool of myself, and he would hurt me anyway.

• Why can't he be a normal dad and love me the way he's supposed to? I'd forgive him and never tell. I want a real dad more than anything.

• Why doesn't Mom see that something is wrong? Mom, can't you see? Please see!

At first I thought it was part of growing up   that this was something all daddies did. I was happy because Daddy was really talking to me for the first time in my life. I'd always wanted that. I thought it was O.K. for him to teach me how to make my husband happy. Until he went too far. I was only eleven. I begged him to stop and pleaded with him not to make me do it, but he wouldn't listen.

Sometimes I would pretend to have accepted it, just so he wouldn't hurt me so bad. Then I felt even more guilty. He'd tell me to do things to myself when I was alone. Later he would ask me if I did. I lied to him out of fear, just so he'd leave me alone. Then I felt guilty for lying. If I told him I hadn't done the gross things he told me to do, he'd force me to do them in front of him.

> I don't want to tell the world. I can't destroy
> the good things people remember about my father.

---

*How you feel about what happened to you affects how
you feel about yourself—and that affects all your
relationships.*

What emotions can you pick out of Joanie's letter? Fear,
confusion, guilt, shame, despair, frustration? You might
want to stop and make a list of the feelings you recognize
as being a result of your own abuse.

■ A Bag Full of Garbage

When a person is sexually abused, it's almost as if the
perpetrator takes a jumbo-sized garbage bag, throws up in
it, gives it to his victim, and tells her to carry it—forever.
And because the victim is afraid and doesn't know what
else to do, she takes it and carries the awful stench and
burden everywhere. With every new experience of abuse,
the perpetrator re-opens the bag and puts in more filth.
What kind of filth? Slimy, decaying emotions, destructive,
putrid lies, and the rotting remains of the parts of us that
the perpetrator has murdered. Finally the bag full of garbage begins to affect the victim. She starts accepting the
lies about herself. As her shame grows, she often begins to
behave in ways that add to that garbage in the bag.

In this book we're going to talk a lot about feelings and
actions. You may be able to express some of your own
feelings for the first time as you read about other girls in

this book who have had trouble with those same feelings. Their stories will help you learn the truth: *those feelings are lying to you about who you are.*

Sorting through
the Trash

6

Scared to Death

THINK FOR A MINUTE ABOUT HOW YOU FELT AT THE TIME of your abuse. Fear was probably the first feeling you experienced.

■ Like a Horror Movie

For a young child, sexual abuse can be something like stepping into a horror movie. The moon rises, you hear an eerie howl, and an ordinary-looking man is transformed into a terrible monster. His facial appearance changes, the voice deepens to a growl, and his breathing becomes heavy and panting. There is always a victim.

The child sexual abuse victim isn't even warned by a full moon or a wolf's howl. An ordinary person, usually someone she knows, is changed without warning, and she is the prey.

I had known Papa as a quiet, gentle, safe person. Then suddenly he came to me in the dark, making confusing demands and hurting me a lot. The transformation was terrifying. It rocked my whole world.

All sexual abuse victims, even those who are older when they were abused and had more information about sex and sexuality, experience fear. There is fear that the secret will get out, fear of not being believed, fear of the results, and fear that others can "see."

■ The Darkest Secret

We sexual abuse victims learned from the very beginning of our abuse that what happened to us was a terrible secret we must keep. Sometimes we were threatened with harm to ourselves or our families.

Peggy and Tommy, brother and sister, were sexually abused and used in pornography by their elderly babysitters. The couple showed the children a rack of guns on their bedroom wall and told the preschoolers they would kill the children's parents and drown the children in the bathtub if they told anyone.

Trudy's father told her that he would kill her mother if Trudy ever told anyone he was abusing her. Since he had been in jail for manslaughter twice before, Trudy had every reason to believe he would keep his word, so the abuse continued for five years. Trudy lived in constant fear for her mother's life. One day when Trudy was taking a shortcut home from a friend's, a drunk man stepped out from behind a tree and attempted to grab her. The incident was Trudy's "last straw." It frightened her so badly that she attempted suicide on the school bus the next morning.

The suicide attempt failed. Trudy asked to see me because she remembered my talk in her school assembly. We'd set up a program in her school called "Dealing with the Effects of Sexual Abuse *Before* You Enter the Real World." Trudy joined the group, and the fearful burden of her secret was lifted. The last I heard, Trudy was college-bound.

Even when an abuser doesn't threaten a victim with harm, he still makes sure she knows that the incident is something she can't talk about—a "special secret" just between the two of them.

But keeping the secret contributes to your fear. And the fear that someone will find out is part of that heavy and putrid heap of trash you're carrying around.

■ Fear that Others Can "See"

Another lie in the bag of garbage a victim carries is that others can tell that you've been abused.

I remember the first meeting of one support group I was leading. The last girl to arrive came in apologizing for being late. About halfway across the room, she stopped and said to the girl directly in front of her, "You can't be sexually abused! We double-dated Friday night!"

That girl believed that *everyone* could tell that she had been abused—and also that she would have been able to tell if the girl she had doubled with had been abused.

My step-mother told me that everyone could tell that I was evil: "You're bad. Everybody knows it!" And then, when the man next door abused me, I was sure it happened because he could "tell" that there was something "wrong" or "bad" in me that made it all right for him to hurt me.

A victim of sex abuse feels very self-conscious about her body because she feels sure that others can "see" that she's been abused. If you've never experienced sexual abuse, you might be thinking, "That's ridiculous! No one could look at a person's body and know she'd been abused." And you're right, no one *can* tell from looking.

But sexual abuse isn't rational. That feeling of being "damaged goods," not worth much, is pervasive in the thinking of an abuse victim. We feel the damage and the separation so deeply that it seems reasonable that anyone should be able to look at us and "see" what happened.

■ Will They Believe Me?

Many victims are afraid that they might not be believed if they tell their stories. Unfortunately, that's a well-founded fear, as Tonya discovered.

Tonya is the most up-front, tell-it-like-it-is person you could ever meet. She has a terrific personality and an exuberant spirit.

Tonya was sixteen when she joined one of my support groups. Here's the story she shared with us:

> You guys know I live with my grandma, but you
> don't know why. I'm there because my grandma
> took me away from my mom. My parents were
> divorced when I was seven. Dad lives in New York.
> I lived with my mom.
>
> My mom doesn't have many friends—not real
> friends, anyway. She goes out to party, but the
> people she meets don't hang around long. She does
> have one good friend, Hannah.

One night when I was twelve, Hannah and her husband came over. I stayed in my room 'cause I hated to watch them drink. Hannah's husband got drunk, came into my room, and lay down in the bed beside me. He said I was beautiful, and he put his hands under my pajama tops. I started to cry. He told me to be quiet, that he wasn't going to hurt me. But he did. When he finished, he said I'd better not tell my mom.

I wanted to go wash the blood off me so bad, but I was afraid to come out of my bedroom. Finally all three of them passed out in the living room. Then I took a shower and changed the sheets on my bed.

I didn't tell anybody. I felt ashamed, and I just wanted to forget it had happened. But Hannah's husband cornered me in the clubhouse of the apartment complex where we lived. He rubbed my breast through my clothes and told me how much he'd enjoyed our "time together" and how he was looking forward to our being alone again.

That really scared me. So I told my mom. And she didn't believe me! Can you believe that? My own mom thought I'd lie to her about a thing like that! She said she didn't ever want to hear another lie like that again. She kept inviting them to our house, and he kept on coming in my room.

Finally I couldn't stand it anymore, so I told my grandma. She was furious! She told Mom she would take her to court as an unfit parent if she didn't sign papers giving me to her. So Mom signed the papers. My grandma took me to a counselor at the middle school. I was uncomfortable with her—

> she was always staring at my hair and my make-up like there was something wrong with the way I looked. I couldn't talk to her because I felt like she already thought I was no good.
>
> Grandma did the best she could, and I didn't want her to worry anymore. At the end of the school year I told Grandma I was fine, that the counselor and I had worked out all my problems. And I didn't do anything else about it until Jan showed up. I lied to Grandma—things are not O.K. for me. But for the first time, I'm starting to think they can be.

Mothers who have been abused and haven't dealt with their own abuse often deny that their children are being abused. We'll talk more about that when we get into mother/daughter relationships.

Being sexually abused is horrendous enough. But when you are abused and then not believed when you seek help, it's even more devastating. If you have told someone about your abuse and that person didn't believe you, do what Tonya did. Tell someone else. Keep telling people until you find someone who will believe you and help you. If you can't find anyone to help, call us at Tree of Rest, Inc. Our toll-free number is in the back of this book.

■ What's Going to Happen to Me?

Remember when the older girls told me that sexual inter-course leads to pregnancy? That was a new fear for me. I didn't know if I would get pregnant, and I didn't know what would happen to me if I did. I was sure that my step-mother and father would be angry and that I would be in big trouble, but I wasn't sure what they'd do to me.

You might feel very afraid of what might happen to you. Maybe you're afraid you'll become pregnant or get a disease. You may live in constant fear that it's going to happen again (and that is a very justifiable fear). You might be afraid people will say awful things or physically abuse you if the truth comes out. You may be afraid you will end up separated from your family.

■ What's Going to Happen to My Family?

Victims of sexual abuse often worry about what's going to happen to their families if the truth comes out.

If the abuser is the father, step-father, or live-in boyfriend of the victim's mother, he often insures the victim's silence by telling her that if she tells, she'll be put in a foster home, he will go to jail, and her mother will go crazy and have to be "put away." That leaves the victim with such thoughts as:

- Mom couldn't take it if she knew. I don't want her to go crazy.

- If my parents get divorced, it will be my fault.

- It'll be all my fault if our family is broken up.

- Mom will kill me if her boyfriend goes to jail!

Even if the abuser is an uncle or brother or cousin, the victim knows that telling will cause problems within the family.

■ A Heavy Responsibility

These are heavy responsibilities for anyone to carry. They are also lies!

> *The responsibility for whatever happens to your family or your abuser belongs to the abuser—ALWAYS AND ONLY.*

It is *never* your fault, no matter who tells you it is!

■ Getting Rid of Some Fears

How secret is your experience of abuse? Have you told anybody? How did your abuser let you know that what he had done to you was a secret?

Getting rid of fear is going to be a tough battle. Just when you've conquered one fear, something else will pop up, and you'll start to be afraid again. At least that's the way it was for me for a long time.

How do you fight such a tough battle? By learning the truth and repeatedly telling yourself the truth. For example, when you go out the door feeling that everyone can tell you are a victim, remind yourself, "No one can really tell I've been abused! That's a lie, and I refuse to believe it!"

Or if someone tells you or makes you feel like you are responsible for keeping your family together, tell yourself the truth. "I'm not responsible for what happens to my family. My abuser is. He's the one who chose to put his desires above the good of the family. He's the guilty one, not me!"

Don't let fear keep you from getting started on your journey through and beyond the effects of sexual abuse. As you make that journey, you'll learn more and more truth about your abuse. As you use the weapon of truth, you'll find yourself winning more and more battles against the fear that has kept you from becoming the real you that you were meant to be.

7

I'm So Confused!

EARLIER YOU MADE A LIST OF SOME OF THE EMOTIONS you felt as a result of your abuse. Was confusion on your list?

Statistics show that in 85 to 90 percent of sexual abuse cases the victim knows the perpetrator. That means the abuser is a relative or a family friend or a person from church or school—someone with whom the victim had some kind of relationship.

For most victims of sexual abuse, the incident or incidents of abuse turn the world as they know it upside down. For children—even for teens—adults are the people who make the rules, build the home, and generally are in charge. Especially for younger kids, adults are the creators of the safe world they live in. The security of that world is shattered when these adults break the rules.

One incest victim named Mandy said, "I didn't know who I was—my dad's little girl or his mistress! One minute

I was being disciplined for not picking up my toys, and the next I was being seduced." Mandy didn't deserve the confusion she felt—neither do you.

Who was your abuser? What was his relationship to you? In what ways did your abuse confuse your world?

■ Sexual Confusion

Part of your confusion is caused by a natural tendency to think of your abuse experience strictly as a sexual event, an event brought about by "something wrong" with who you are that caused someone else to have sexual feelings and behave sexually toward you.

But sexual abuse is not a "sexual" issue for your abuser. His problems are usually rooted in the need for power and control born out of a fear of rejection. His reasons for the abuse don't have much to do with sex at all, except that sex is the means he uses to demonstrate power and exercise control. Since children and teens are more accepting than adults, he feels more power and can exercise more control over children and teens.

> *How do you feel about your own sexuality? About sex? Can you think of some emotions or attitudes you have about your own sexuality that came from your experience of abuse?*

■ "I Love You—I Hate You!"

Another area of confusion for many of us victims is that we often still love our abusers. That's hard for people who haven't been abused to understand. But often we had close relationships with the perpetrators before the abuse began, and it's not unusual for an abuser to show his victim even more attention and affection during the time of abuse.

A child doesn't stop loving someone just because that someone hurt him or her. Children are accepting and forgiving and believe that the people they love are "good."

After my step-grandfather abused me, I knew I couldn't trust him anymore, but I still loved him. I loved him because I thought he loved me, and I needed to be loved. I couldn't understand why a "good" person like Papa would do something bad like that to me. I felt he must have an excellent reason for hurting me. Out of my confusion I learned to blame myself for my abuse.

How do you feel about your abuser? Have you felt confused because you sometimes feel love for your abuser?

Do you sometimes feel that your life is so confused and "messed up" that there's no way it will ever be right? Well, I've got good news for you. The problems and confusion we've talked about in this chapter can be overcome. It won't be easy; it'll be a lot of hard work. But living with it sure hasn't been easy either, has it? You've had to put a lot of effort into just surviving. Now it's time to put your effort into learning the truth and using the truth to overcome the lies of abuse.

8

I Feel So Guilty

GUILT IS A FEELING OF PAIN ABOUT SOMETHING
you've done. Even though you might not have had the
words to define it, you've probably felt plenty of guilt
yourself. I've never met a sexual abuse victim who hasn't.

Think back to the time of your abuse. Then think about
how you feel about your abuse now. Do you feel guilty for
any part of what happened?

■ Sherry's Story

I want to introduce you to Sherry, a teen friend of mine
whose experience of abuse might help you recognize the lie
that you are guilty of your abuse.

Sherry was sixteen when I first met her in a support
group for girls who had been sexually abused. She has
golden-brown hair and light-brown eyes that seem to have

flecks of gold in them. She has a nice figure, and I think she's a gorgeous young lady.

By the time our group met for the second time, Sherry was having nightmares almost every night. Dumping the lies and garbage of sexual abuse had meant digging deep into her reservoir of guilt and shame, and it was almost too much for her to bear.

"I wish I could go back to before you came here!" she cried out at me. "At least I didn't think about it much then, and I sure hadn't dreamed about it in a long time!"

"I'm sorry, Sherry," I answered her. "I know that opening the garbage bag lets out the stench—and sometimes that makes us gag. I wish there were another way to get it out because I know this hurts. Do you want to share what happened with us? We want to be here for you and help you through this."

"No, I don't want to share what I'm feeling! I want to *stop* feeling what I'm feeling! I just want to forget. It was the stupidest thing I've ever done, and I just want to forget it. Why can't it just die?" But as she was speaking, the anger in Sherry's voice changed to desperation. "But I'm going to tell."

Sherry knew that the memories of her abuse were not going to die, and the painful feelings were not going to go away. She knew she had to talk about her experience to get it out.

Most of you were attacked by someone, but I was different—I really did cause my own problems. I was so anxious to be grown up that I arranged to have sex on my fourteenth birthday. I asked a six-teen-year-old boy in my neighborhood to take me out and have sex with me. But when the petting

64

got heavy, I wanted to stop. But he wouldn't. I haven't spoken to him since that night.

I didn't tell anyone for a long time. I felt disgusting—dirty and ashamed. Then I told my mom. She was so disappointed with me because I planned to have sex that she wouldn't talk to me for the rest of the day. Later, she told me she would help me if I wanted to prosecute the guy, but I couldn't.

I have a boyfriend now, but if he ever found out about "X," he'd never want to touch me again. I call him "X" because I don't think he deserves a name. He hurt me, and he took away part of my life, so I'm taking away his name.

■ Sherry's Problem

> *How do you feel about Sherry's story? To you, does it seem like the abuse was Sherry's fault or her abuser's fault?*

It is true that sometimes guys have a hard time understanding that *no* means no. In some ways our culture has taught guys to think that girls don't really mean it when they say it. They sometimes think we say no because it's what we're supposed to say, but that what we really want is for them to be strong and forceful. I know it seems ridiculous, but our society has talked about and portrayed guy-girl relationships in a way that leaves this impression.

But—and this is important to remember—that never makes it all right for anyone to force you to have sex.

65

Sherry's abuse experience was not her fault. Sherry was a victim; a crime was perpetrated against her. Her abuser ignored her wishes and violated her body. He made the decision. The responsibility for the abuse belongs *always and only* to the abuser!

Look at it this way. Let's say Sherry worked for a large corporation in a big city and she planned with a coworker to embezzle money from the corporation. But at the last minute, Sherry changed her mind and refused to go through with it. Her coworker would have no right to put a gun to her head and force her to steal the money anyway.

Yes, Sherry made a stupid move in pursuing a sexual encounter. But Sherry had never heard the truth about real love and beautiful sexuality. She knew very little about what sex truly is. Sherry was foolish to ask for something she didn't really understand just to try to be grown up, but that was a mistake. The physical violence of abuse was not her fault. Sherry would never have chosen such pain and fear.

■ Megan's Story

Megan is seventeen, and she has dark blue eyes. Not long ago, she was raped by the husband of her best friend. Since her parents realized the importance of counseling for victims of rape, Megan was already in individual counseling when she joined our group. Here is her story, as she shared it with the girls in the group.

> My best friend isn't a high-school student. Sandy's older, and she's married. A few months ago I dropped by her house on my way to work. I work nights at a nursing home, and I used to visit Sandy

66

two or three times a week. Sandy's shift at her job was usually over by 3:00 in the afternoon. That day, when I got there, Sandy's husband, Ron, said she had to stay late but that she'd be home any minute.

So I went in the house and watched some TV with Ron while I waited. Ron was drinking beer. I didn't drink anything—I was on my way to work. Ron told me I was pretty. I told him where to put his compliments. I figured he'd been drinking more than I realized. It didn't bother me much—I'd often seen him drinking lots of times. So I wasn't afraid.

All of a sudden he sort of pounced on me—like a cat. He put his hand inside my shirt and started licking my face.

I screamed at him, shoving him and swearing at him, but I couldn't get him away from me. Ron is huge—he works out a lot, so he's really strong.

I almost got away once, but he grabbed me from behind and carried me into their bedroom. He threw me down. I scratched his face, and he slapped me. He threatened to break my neck.

When it was over, he told me I wasn't as good as he thought I'd be. He said he thought I'd fight him harder. He told me to get up and go to work. "Sandy won't be home 'til midnight. I'll tell her you stopped by," he said as I walked out the door.

I was numb. I wanted to take a bath, but I couldn't go home. I didn't know what to do. I drove around until it was time to go to work. My boss took one look at me and knew something was wrong. When she tried to talk to me, I started to

67

cry and throw up. When she heard what happened, she wanted to call the police. But I didn't want her to because my dad is a criminal attorney and knows all the policemen. She called anyway.

The police took me to the hospital and called my mom and dad. They went and picked up Ron. Sandy had just gotten home. At first she didn't believe what the police were telling her. She came to the police station with Ron. When she saw me she started to cry and say, "I'm sorry, I'm sorry."

They kept Ron in jail until the next afternoon. The police wanted me to press charges, but I didn't want to because of Dad. Mom and Dad said it was up to me. Dad told me not to worry about him, but I knew it would be hard on him. So the —— is still out there walking around.

After he got out of jail, Ron told Sandy I had come over and seduced him. He said I scratched him because he said I wasn't as good at sex as Sandy is. And Sandy believed him! She thinks it was as much my fault as Ron's. She moved out because Ron had been unfaithful to her—not because he raped me! That——is telling everyone that I wanted him to—

Megan was not crying as she told her story. She was fighting mad. She wanted to prove Ron was lying about her, but she didn't want to hurt her dad.

Eventually, Megan did decide to prosecute. She found that she couldn't get past the shame until she could prove legally that she had not consented to the sexual encounter.

Megan did not want either of her parents in the courtroom. She didn't feel she could handle the strain of having them hear exactly what had been done to her. I was permitted to sit with her at the prosecution table. She even stayed at my house during the beginning of the trial. It's often difficult for victims to face the people whose approval they need most, even if there is no rejection to worry about. It was just plain hard for Megan to be with her parents during this time.

Megan had an almost painful grip on my hand as we waited for the judge's verdict. When he said, "Guilty," Megan broke down for the first time. All the anger that had been her survival mechanism melted away in tears of relief. She had proved to the whole world that *her abuser was guilty* and *she was not!*

Now Megan is attending a local college, where she's studying nursing. I ran into her not long ago and she said, "You know, I'm going to forgive that jerk yet. I can feel it coming!" It was great to hear her laughing. She told me, "Life is good, you know?"

Megan isn't dating anyone right now. "All my energy goes to schoolwork!" she said. And that's all right. Not everyone dates or marries. But every person needs to feel comfortable with her sexuality because only then can she learn to give and accept true love from the people in her life.

■ It Must Be My Fault

Sherry felt guilty because she had arranged to have sex. Megan knew in her head that she wasn't guilty, but she still needed to prove it before she could be free. Someone else feels guilty because she's been told she's sexy. I felt guilty because I sat in my step-grandfather's lap. Some even feel guilty just because they can't blame their abuser.

> *Do you feel as if your abuse was your fault? What do you think you did or didn't do that makes you guilty?*

Don't listen to the lie that your abuse must be your fault. Fight it with the truth. Remind yourself, "I didn't choose this! My abuser stole from me!" Remind yourself that your abuser's distortions led him to make a choice to involve you in his perversion. Always remember: *The guilt for abuse belongs always and only to the abuser. The victim is never guilty!*

9

Struggling with Shame

I CAN'T COUNT THE TIMES GIRLS WHO HAVE BEEN SEX-ually abused asked me questions like, "Why me?" "What's wrong with me?" "Why didn't I make him stop?" "Why did I let it happen again?" All of the questions are connected to one word: *shame*. Shame is the real monster, the emotion you and I have felt and will go to almost any lengths to avoid feeling. Shame says it's not O.K. to be me.

Shame is the name for your persistent belief that you are "bad" or "evil." Shame makes you think you deserve abuse. Shame makes you blame yourself for all the terrifying and painful and disappointing events in your life.

■ Not What You Do, But Who You Are

Shame is the horribly painful sense that you are guilty of something that has lowered you in character or morals,

71

something that has brought you into contempt or dishonor. It is a feeling of intense pain about *who you are*. Shame is a lie that covers up the real you and causes you to see a "dirty" or "guilty" person in your place.

Shame doesn't say that what you did was bad. After all, anybody can—at least in her mind—understand that at times everyone behaves in a wrong or inappropriate manner. No, shame is much more destructive than that. Shame says that *who you are* is bad.

Undeserved shame (and all the shame you feel about your abuse is undeserved) *is the most self-destructive emotion sexual abuse victims have to deal with.* If we want to stop feeling guilt, we stop *doing* the things that make us feel guilty. But to stop shame, we have to stop *being* who we are because it's who we are that causes us shame.

It's shame that makes us feel like we're damaged goods: "I might as well sleep around—I'm used anyway. Nobody good will ever want me." Shame makes us accept the guilt for our abuse: "Something is wrong with me or he wouldn't have picked me."

Even when we've expressed our shame through anger and hatred for our abuser, the underlying reason for our anger and hatred is that he made us "feel so dirty."

Shame makes us dislike who we are sexually. We were created as sexual beings with sexual feelings. But if shame isn't dealt with, it inhibits our ability to enjoy sex as it was intended to be. With shame, we learn to hate or fear sexuality. And when real love arrives, we can't share our sexuality or our feelings because shame tells us they are bad.

Shame also keeps us from getting help because in order to get help, we have to tell someone else who we think we are. We feel this way: "I can't tell you who I am because if you knew who I am, you wouldn't like me. I know because I know who I am, and *I* don't like me." But the sad truth is that *we really don't know who we are.*

> *Shame goes beyond not allowing us to expose ourselves to others—it hides the truth of our real selves from ourselves!*

■ Mary's Story

A girl came up to talk with me after I'd lectured at her school. "Can I bring my friend to talk to you?" she asked. "I think she's been abused." She was right.

Mary told me that she'd been sexually abused by her father ever since she could remember. When she was real little and it hurt her, her dad stuffed his dirty socks in her mouth to keep her from crying out. As she grew older, he told her he loved her, that she was his favorite, and that this was a special secret between them. He said she was so sexy he just couldn't keep his hands off her, that she made him want her. He assured her that fathers were supposed to teach their daughters about sex and that there was something wrong with her if she didn't enjoy it.

Because Mary was sexually stimulated at such a young age and for such a long period of time, she learned to experience a great deal of pleasure. Eventually, she told her dad that she was sorry she'd been so much trouble, and that he was right. Thinking it was perfectly normal, she began to help her father find times and places when they could be together. He praised her for becoming such a very good daughter.

73

When Mary started junior-high school, she found out that fathers were *not* supposed to have sex with their daughters. Because of her cooperation with her father, she told me, "I feel like I've been seducing my father all my life!" So one night she slashed her wrist—and her face and her chest—with a razor blade.

Mary was hospitalized and treated for attempted suicide, but she didn't mention the abuse. Neither did her father. After she was released and sent home, the abuse began again. Mary ran away—five times. Every time she was found, brought home, and abused again.

Finally, she was judged to be an "incorrigible child" (one who can't be reformed), made a ward of the court, and placed in a state foster home. The court ordered her entire family into counseling.

At the time when I met Mary, her family had been in counseling once a week for six years. And in all that time, no one had ever mentioned the sexual abuse!

■ You Didn't Give Permission

Mary's story may seem hard to believe, but it's not when you understand the damage done to a human being who has had her body stimulated without her informed consent, against her will, and out of her control. The shame of not being able to control the responses of her own body spoke volumes to Mary about who she was—and none of it was good.

This lie that "somewhere deep down inside I must have wanted this to happen to me, or I wouldn't have felt pleasure" is devastating. We need to understand that our bodies are made to respond is specific ways "when the right buttons are pushed." Any pleasure we experienced had nothing to do with our initial wishes.

> *Receiving pleasure does not mean you wanted sexual contact or gave your abuser permission!*

Unfortunately, there are some people who will take advantage of that feeling of shame to pressure an abuse victim into a sexual relationship. Marla was attacked as a teenager, and at first her boyfriend was really supportive. "We got really close afterwards," she said. "But I could tell he felt I was worth less than before the attack. We became a steady thing, and he wanted to jump right into sex. I didn't even want him to touch me, but he said I didn't have the right to pull that 'Ms. Purity' act with him because he knew about the attack. He said if I could do it with a stranger, then he should be no problem. I was fourteen when we became lovers."

Marla's boyfriend reinforced the damage done by her attacker and added some damage of his own. Instead of helping Marla to see that the ugliness and shame belonged to her abuser and not at all to her, Marla's boyfriend preyed on her sense of being "damaged goods" and used the wound as a way to get her to satisfy his own sexual desires. Marla's hurt was deep, but her boyfriend made it much deeper by telling her that her shame was true when it was really false.

Shame is the monster sexual abuse victims face. But that monster can be defeated as you learn to accept the truth that *the shame attached to abuse belongs always and only to the abuser—never to the victim.*

You might not believe it yet, but you *can* get through and beyond the shame of abuse. The answer lies in throwing out the lie (that you are bad or not worth loving or that you deserve abuse) and in learning that the real you is truly valuable and worthy to receive the real kind of love we'll be talking about later.

10

I Hate You!

KIM IS TALL, WITH DEEP BLUE EYES AND SHINY BROWN hair. And she is full of hatred for both her parents.

> I hate my parents more for what they did to my sister Kay than for what they did to me. Dad abused her for eight years. Even in front of other people, Dad would grab her and hug her, rubbing her body up against him. Kay was embarrassed. Kay did tell Mom what Dad was doing to her, and Mom told Kay it was her fault. Mom said, "If you'd stop acting so sexy and stay away from him, he'd leave you alone."
>
> My grandmother found out about it. She tried to prosecute my dad, but he got off.

> Kay finally ran away. Now she's married to a guy
> who's so jealous he hits her if anybody looks at her.
> I'm so scared he's going to hurt her bad one day.
>
> My dad never liked me. He wanted a boy when
> I was born. He kept telling me that. But as soon as
> Kay left the house, he started tickling me and play-
> ing with my legs. I told him how much I hated him.
> I said I'd kill him if he didn't leave me alone. So far
> he has.
>
> But I'm scared to be in the same house with
> him. I try to stay awake until I'm sure he's asleep.
> He is really crazy. One night at the dinner table he
> actually told us he wanted to die in jail on a rape
> charge. Mom just looked at him. They deserve each
> other. I hate them both.

Kim wasn't crying or hysterical when she expressed her
hatred for her parents. She was quite calm, sure in her
anger. Kim's dad is really a sick person—in his mind and
in his actions—and for years Kim's mother has neglected
to step in to protect her children. Kim's anger at her parents
is very understandable.

---

*Do you hate the person who abused you? Do you hate
the person you feel didn't protect you?*

It's very common to hear abuse victims express intense
hatred or a desire to kill the perpetrators of abuse.

But is this hatred good for us? Here's what happened
one day in a support group of abuse victims (you know some

of them), when we'd been talking about how much we hated our abusers.

■ Is This Good for Us?

"Is this good for us?" asked Christy. "I mean, here we are, sitting around talking about how much we hate. Are you sure we ought to be doing this?"

"Why shouldn't we? It's what we feel, and we're supposed to talk about how we feel," Tonya answered her. "Right?"

The girls looked at me.

"Yes, we *are* supposed to talk about how we feel," I answered. "And hate is a legitimate feeling. Each of you has a right to be experiencing that feeling. And yes, it's better to get in touch with your feelings of hate than to keep them buried or pretend they don't exist. But what Christy is getting at is that it's not good for us to get stuck in the hate."

"So what do we do about it?" asked Christy.

"Well, we start by looking at hate and how it affects us and then we choose whether or not we want to continue feeling that way."

"Choose?" emphasized Christy. "That seems pretty obvious—we aren't supposed to hate."

"Why not?" I asked.

"Because we're just not supposed to."

"But why aren't we supposed to?" I kept pushing.

Christy was getting frustrated. "I don't know!"

"Because hate isn't good for us." Kim spoke the words with the same calm, matter-of-fact voice she used to tell us how she hated her parents.

"Right!" I exclaimed. "It isn't good for *us*—the ones doing the hating. I remember the day I took a good look at myself and saw a woman whose life was being controlled by a man in prison. I thought, 'That guy doesn't care about me. He doesn't care how I feel about him. Hating him is wrecking my life, and he doesn't even care!' Think about it. How about you, Megan? Does hating Sam hurt him or even make him feel bad?"

"No!" Megan admitted. "But it sure makes me feel better."

"It makes me angry," offered Sherry. "The more I think about how much I hate him, the angrier I get."

"And what do you do with the anger?" I asked. "I mean, do you act on your anger? Do you go out and get the guy—do something hateful to your abuser?"

"No, there's nothing I *can* do to him," said Sherry. "I guess I just keep the hate and anger inside."

"I don't. Usually I do something rotten to my little sister," confessed Tonya.

"Yeah, I guess that happens to me, too," Sherry said thoughtfully. "Only it would be my mom, since she's the one I'm around most."

"Then how do you feel?" I asked.

"Like a slimeball," said Tonya with her usual candor. "I do love the kid—sometimes I don't know why I treat her so mean."

"So even though Tonya and Sherry hate their abusers and are angry with them, they sometimes take it out on somebody else. What about the rest of you—does that happen to you?"

Every girl in the group admitted to feeling guilty about taking out her hate and anger on innocent people.

"So how do we stop?" Tonya almost begged for an answer. "I've tried to stop on my own, and I can't."

■ So How Do We Stop?

The girls discovered something important that day: that getting stuck in the hate and anger hurt only *them* and not the people who abused them. They also found that when they kept that hurt and anger inside, it sometimes spilled over and affected other people they really cared about.

> *What about you? Does your anger make you feel better? Or does it just make you more angry and hard to be around?*

Think about the hate and anger you feel now toward your abuser or toward others who have hurt you. Do your feelings affect your abuser in any way? Can you see ways in which your feelings are hurting *you*? Do you want to keep the anger and hate, or give it up?

Deciding to give up the hurt and anger is only the beginning, of course. Like everything else in our journey through and beyond abuse, it takes time and hard work. But most of the girls in our group wanted to stop hurting others and themselves with their anger. They wanted to know, "So how do we stop?"

Most of them didn't like the answer I gave them: *"The only way to get rid of hate and anger is to forgive the people who have hurt you."* For me, that meant forgiving the man who battered and raped me and the people who had caused so much hurt in my childhood.

Most of the girls said "Never!" at first. Probably you feel that way, too. But maybe it will help to clarify what forgiveness really means.

■ Real Forgiveness

Forgiveness doesn't mean that you say, "What you did to me was O.K." Abuse is *never* O.K. Forgiveness is exactly the opposite. *Real* forgiveness acknowledges that someone *has* done something wrong, but it also means that you're not going to make them pay the penalty for their wrong.

Now that *does not* mean a perpetrator shouldn't be prosecuted legally. I believe sex abusers should be prosecuted for two reasons. One is *to keep others from being abused by them.* Sexual crimes are the most often repeated crimes there are because sexual abusers do not stop abusing unless they're forced to stop. The second reason is *to get help for the sex abusers themselves.* Abusers will not stay in counseling or any program designed to help them unless they're forced by law, so that is not the part of the penalty that can be forgiven.

No, the penalty a sexual abuser *can* be forgiven is the penalty of our anger and hatred. Abusers deserve both penalties: they've earned them both. But we need to give up the penalty of our hatred and anger toward them—for our own sakes.

The truth is that victims who forgive their abusers move through their abuse more quickly, and that's what is important to me. But don't feel terrible if you can't forgive your abuser in one day. I wouldn't expect that. Just *think* about it. Give the idea a chance—for your own sake.

11

Innocence Lost

SEXUAL ABUSE ENDED YOUR CHILDHOOD. SECURITY, peace, comfort, an atmosphere of learning and growing— all those aspects of childhood hinge on a child's ability to trust the adult makers of her world. When that trust is broken, childhood dies. When it happened to you, suddenly you knew more about pain, guilt, shame, betrayal, and sex than anyone should know.

■ Teresa's Story

Let me introduce you to Teresa, who you'll get to know throughout this book.

Teresa was sixteen when she joined a support group I was leading at her local YWCA. Underneath her mop of wild black hair, her face was truly pretty. She wore clothes that made her look seductive. Teresa had been abused by her teenaged cousin Mike the summer she was eight. As Teresa began to understand the truth about the results of her abuse, she felt a need to confront Mike. I was there for the encounter.

"You hurt me!" she exploded. "I was only eight years old, and I loved you. But you kept hurting me. And then it stopped hurting, and I started to like it. I wanted you to do it to me. Then you went away, but I kept thinking about you coming back and doing it to me. When I was only eleven years old, I was running around my elementary school looking for boys to do it to me! I shouldn't even have known what it was, Mike!" There was a pleading quality in her voice as she tried to make him understand how much damage the knowledge he forced on her had done to her.

"I'm a slut, Mike! You made me a slut!" Then her voice took on real determination and strength. "Well, no more slut, Mike! No more slut!"

■ Too Much Too Soon

Teresa put into words a sad and often destructive truth about sexual abuse victims. We all know things we shouldn't know. But for all we do know, there's still so much we don't know.

As an abused child or young person, you probably didn't know what to do with your new, unwanted knowledge of sex. You didn't know how to protect yourself. You didn't know how to stop the pain and guilt and fear. You didn't know how to cover your shame. And, worst of all, you didn't know the truth about yourself or real love and sexuality.

When I was eighteen years old, I ran away from my alcoholic home. My father was furious, and he tried to have me extradited (brought back legally) from the state I'd run to. He wanted to have me placed in a mental institution. I didn't think I was crazy, so I agreed to see a psychiatrist. I promised to go home if the doctor said I should be hospitalized. After all the testing, the doctor told me that my real problem was only that I was nineteen and had never been allowed to be nine.

Everybody needs to be nine, and ten, and eleven—or five or six. Everybody needs to have a chance to live in innocent childhood. But that wasn't possible for you and me. Our childhoods were forcefully taken from us. Not only did we lose childhood, we weren't even given the opportunity to mourn the loss.

■ Mourning the Loss

Have you lost a grandmother or grandfather or a friend you loved? It's hard to deal with that kind of loss. Some of us keep expecting that loved one to come walking through the door, smiling and talking the same as ever. We wish it could happen so much that we act as if it really were going to be that way. Others of us avoid the topic of death, holding back the tears and not dealing with the subject at all.

We abuse survivors sometimes respond to the death of our childhoods in much the same way. We work like crazy to make life the way it was before the abuse or to make it the way we wish it could be. We want to find the children we once were and "fix" the world for them. Some of us refuse even to admit that something has died. We pretend we haven't lost anything, so we don't need to mourn.

Have you grieved your loss of childhood?

85

As a child sexual abuse victim, you need to grieve over the loss of your childhood just the way you mourn when someone you care about dies.

People mourn in different ways—some get angry, some cry, some do both. No matter how you mourn the loss of your childhood, it's important that you acknowledge your hurt. Don't be afraid of your anger—being angry over what has been done to you is perfectly normal and acceptable. And don't be ashamed to cry: crying over the pain can help you get through your sexual abuse into a healthy view of yourself and relationships. You can't accept the full truth about your abuse until you mourn the loss of the child who died believing the lies. So allow yourself whatever time it takes to get through your grieving process.

■ Getting Past My Loss

It wasn't until I'd gone through enough healing to be able to love someone that I was forced to deal with the death of my childhood.

A deeply caring, wonderfully patient man with an astonishing intuitiveness had come into my life, and I was beginning to love him. But something was wrong, and I couldn't figure out what. I was terrified.

I remember sitting in the office of a valued friend and adviser and saying to him, "I don't know what in the world is wrong with me, Larry." Suddenly I started to cry, and the words came pouring out. "All I ever wanted was to grow up and fall in love and not know there could be all that pain associated with love and sex. It's not fair! I just wanted to grow up like everybody else. That's not too much to ask!"

"But you can't." Larry's voice was quiet and full of compassion. "Part of you died when you were abused. Your childhood died. What you have to do now is let yourself grieve for that death."

My sorrow turned to anger. "But that's not fair! I didn't do anything!" I hit the top of Larry's desk with my fist. "I don't want to think about what sex did to me or what I did with sex. Not now that Norm's in my life! I want it to be like it should be. That's not much to want! I don't want to know how much it can hurt. I just want to forget it all and be in love like an ordinary woman! I should have been able to grow up and discover love and learn about sex with the person I love. It's not supposed to be this way!"

Larry agreed. Then he told me it was O.K. for me to be sad and angry. He told me to go ahead and shout it out—he even said it was O.K. for me to be angry and shout at God. "Go ahead, let it out. Be angry. Feel it instead of burying it. God can take it. God will understand, and he will still love you."

And he was right. I ranted and raved and shouted at God for several days. I beat my pillow with my fist and hollered that it wasn't fair that I was abused, that it wasn't fair that my childhood had died such a terrible death. Then one morning I woke up and I wasn't angry anymore. I was only sad for the child who had been murdered by the lies. I cried for my childhood the way some people cry over the death of someone they love. And when the tears finally stopped, I knew that it was O.K. for me to be an adult in love with a good man.

■ Your Story Hasn't Ended

Maybe, like Teresa, your early experience with sex introduced you to sexual desire long before its time, and you sought casual sex with many partners. The truth is that you can still experience love and sex together as they were intended to be—a wonderful celebration to be shared with the one person you commit yourself to for the rest of your life.

Even if you feel that you lost all sexual innocence when you were abused, the truth is that you are still beautiful and valuable. You were not the perpetrator; you were the victim. Even though you may not believe it now, as you journey into the light of the truth, you'll see that you really *are* worthy of being cherished and loved.

12

Who Can I Trust?

IT PROBABLY DOESN'T SURPRISE YOU THAT TRUST IS A big problem for victims of sexual abuse. After all, if the people you thought you were safe with will hurt you, then who can you trust?

■ Is Anybody Worth Trusting?

Consider this excerpt from a letter written by a victim to her uncle who abused her:

> What you did to me changed the way I thought the opposite sex thought of women. I had no idea that men and boys didn't think of female genitals all the time. I grew up thinking that was always on their minds. You betrayed my trust not only in yourself but in all males through my life.

Obviously, being abused by a person you know and have trusted damages your ability to trust.

Sometimes men who are new at abuse and haven't learned to rationalize their actions will apologize, admit they were wrong, and promise they'll never do it again. Of course, the child believes him even though she has been hurt. But then it happens again, and again, and *again*—until she finally knows it isn't going to stop.

So it's easy to see how being abused causes us to lose our trust in men. But, all too often, victims learn they can't trust their non-abusive parent to protect them either.

■ Christy's Story

Christy was also sixteen when I first met her. Her short blonde hair and athletic build made me guess that she would be pretty good at volleyball and softball. I was right—she was on both teams at her school.

When she was only seven, Christy was molested by her older brother. Then for about two months, her step-father sexually abused her three times a week. The step-father had been abusing her older sister, Emily, for a long time. Emily even had a child by her step-father. But their mother hadn't done anything about confronting or prosecuting their step-father because he was a terminal cancer patient. Christy couldn't even trust the one person who was supposed to protect her from further abuse—her mother.

■ Can I Trust Me?

Sometimes it seems like there's no one a victim can count on. Even the people who don't abuse can't be trusted to provide protection. Often a victim doesn't feel she can even trust herself.

A girl who is older at the time of her first abuse may have known and trusted the man who abused her for a long time. Yet she hadn't been able to tell he was going to hurt her. She may not believe that all men are abusers, but she doesn't believe she can trust her ability to tell which ones are.

Some victims, like Mary, experienced pleasure during their abuse. These girls don't feel like they can trust even their own bodies not to betray them.

Look at the dilemma that not being able to trust anyone, even yourself, puts you in. If you can't trust yourself or other people enough to let anyone get close to you, you can't build friendships or dating relationships. As a matter of fact, you can't build *any* kind of relationship.

■ Journeying toward Trust

As you begin to learn the truth about your abuse, you'll be able to see that all people aren't untrustworthy. And as you continue in your journey, you'll eventually trust yourself enough to pick out one trustworthy person to develop an honest relationship with. And over a period of time, you'll discover that, more often than not, you can tell who is and who isn't trustworthy.

> *Can you believe there will come a time in your life when you'll be able to trust again?*

Don't feel bad if, right now, you can't imagine trusting *anybody* again. Until it started to happen to me, no one could have told me I'd *ever* trust anyone—*especially* a man—again in my whole life! But I did—and, somewhere along your journey, you will too!

13

The Control Game

THE NEED TO BE IN CONTROL IS THE SINGLE MOST important issue in the lives of abuse victims. Even a small child can learn that when someone else is in control, control can hurt. Even a small child can learn that the only way to be sure she won't be hurt again is never to let others be in control.

■ In Control

Most of the time we don't have any idea why we act the way we do! We don't realize that—subconsciously—control has become the motivating factor in our lives.

There are lots of ways to control other people. Some victims become bossy and aggressive, always ready to fight. They behave outrageously and dare anyone to criticize them. They send a message with their attitude: "Nothing can get to me!" They wear plastic faces that are hard and unyielding, but behind those masks the pain is nearly unbearable. For sexual abuse victims, *tough* and *hard-headed* can be just other names for "control."

JoAnn and Missy

JoAnn and Missy hated each other. They were well known in their high school for their hostile behavior toward each other. A good day for them would be to hurl insults and obscenities instead of books as they passed in the school hallway.

When I came to their school and opened support groups for abuse survivors, JoAnn and Missy were in the same group. Others in the group knew them and held their breath while they waited for the explosion. The meeting didn't go very well . . . the air was charged with electricity.

I asked both girls to stay after the group dismissed. It turned out that each girl had experienced similar sexual abuse. Their reactions, in emotions and actions, were almost identical. And to make matters worse, they were both attracted to the same type of guy, so they were often competing. JoAnn and Missy were two angry people who kept butting heads as each tried desperately to control her life.

I spent about an hour trying to explain why they were having so much trouble, but neither wanted to admit to being like the other in any way. Since they both wanted to stay in the group, they agreed to try to make allowances for each other. But they left the room assuring me they would never like each other.

All night I wondered if I should have moved one of them to another group. I worried whether potential blow-ups between the two would slow down the progress of the other girls in the group.

The next afternoon, one of the school counselors called me. He said he'd been interrupted all morning by students who wanted to know what had happened to JoAnn and Missy. They were shocked that instead of throwing objects or obscenities, the girls were passing one another with a simple "hi" and going quietly into their classes.

The counselor was happy, but I knew their newfound compassion for each other would have lots of tests to face as they fought their separate battles with control.

■ Other Ways to Control

Other abuse survivors become submissive or whining, al most to the point of babyish behavior. These people are doormats, and the message they send is: "Go ahead. Walk all over me!" This type of controller will apologize when kicked in the shins, saying, "Oh, did you hurt your foot? Kick me in the stomach next time—it's softer!" Yet apologies and tears can be a way to control, too.

Victims often feel so fatalistic and helpless that they have resigned themselves to being abused. The only control they feel they have is to control when or how their abuse will occur.

Some victims control by regulating every minute of their lives, scheduling every moment. They don't like to do anything that hasn't been planned.

But being controlling isn't exactly behavior that's conducive to winning friends and influencing people. That's one reason sexual abuse victims often don't have good peer relationships.

97

■ Putting Up Walls

One form of control that all abuse victims use to some extent is putting up walls around themselves.

An abuse victim knows quite well how much another person can hurt her, so she begins to build a "fortress" to protect herself, to prevent anyone from getting close enough to hurt her again. She chooses gigantic blocks to construct her walls—blocks too heavy to be pulled down, too smooth to be climbed. She builds the walls high, and she circles herself in completely. And for a while she may feel safe.

But if you try to build a fortress, you're only working against yourself. Before long you'll discover the horrible truth that what you thought you were leaving outside the wall you have actually brought inside with you. And you haven't built a fortress at all. Instead you've built a prison where you are locked inside with all the pain, guilt, shame, and memories you were trying to protect yourself from.

■ Sandy's Story

Sandy is a teenage victim who built a prison of silence, hardness, and alcohol. As a senior in high school, she wrote the following letter to me during her spring break:

> Jan,
>
> I wish I could open up and talk. I feel the need to talk but I don't know what about. I'm afraid of crying. That shows weakness. I am not weak. I'm supposed to be a tough person—that's the only way

I know to survive in this world. I have had a lot of dreams go down the drain, and it really hurts me a lot. So I act tough and handle situations badly. I guess I need support, guidance, and discipline in certain areas of my life. But I don't know how to get out of this prison. How do I get my life on the road again? I don't want to stay drunk for the rest of my life just so I don't remember.

When Sandy came home, she took some positive steps to begin tearing down her walls. She joined a support group and began to see a private counselor one on one. Today she's in her second year of college and is often the designated driver for her group of friends because she doesn't drink anymore.

It's hard work to break down prison walls, and it also takes time. But it can be done—and it's well worth the effort. Sandy would tell you that.

■ Giving Up Control

Do you find yourself nervous in new situations or relationships? Does it scare you to get close to people or to try something new? Is routine important to you—keeping to a schedule, having clear directions and expectations for all activities, etc.? Does it worry you when someone else is "in charge"? *These situations make you uncomfortable because you're not in control.*

Norm has helped me get loose from the control I exercised in various areas of my life by accepting me as I am and giving me time and space to discover and deal with certain areas of my abuse. For example, I discovered another buried area about a month ago. When I told Norm about it, he said that he had been praying for me about that for a year.

"Well, isn't it nice that God finally answered your prayer?" I teased him.

He just laughed and said, "Remember, I know you. It'll take God another three years to get it through to you! But I'm patient."

Norm was telling me he had known all along that I still had to deal with this area of my abuse and that I could have all the time I needed to work through it.

Norm also allows me to control what and how much I tell him about my abuse and how it makes me act. He has never demanded that I share anything with him. He just accepted me as I was until I learned he could be trusted with even my darkest thoughts and deepest feelings. Then he let me share those with him whenever I was ready. By not trying to take control from me, he allowed me freedom to give it away.

"I can't control anything anymore!" I yelled at him one day when I was particularly frustrated.

He just looked at me and laughed. "That's not so bad for someone who used to control everything."

And of course I had to laugh with him because he was right!

Giving up control will probably be one of your toughest struggles. It certainly has been mine! But as you make your journey, you'll learn the truth: you don't have to control every situation. Most people are trustworthy and won't hurt you. That discovery will allow you to start taking down your fortress of control slowly, block by block. And when you've torn down your fortress, you'll be free to experience real love and develop lasting relationships.

14

Sex without the Love

ALL OF US WHO HAVE BEEN SEXUALLY ABUSED HAVE experienced a perversion of sex. We've experienced *sex without love*. Real sex—the way it's intended to be—can only exist inside real love. And real love would never abuse, would never take advantage.

Unfortunately, because of our experiences, many of us mistake sexual abuse for sex. Before most of us even had a chance to learn the truth concerning what sexuality is all about and what sex is supposed to be, we were taught about sex from a painful, devastating experience. And that experience taught us the lie that sex and our sexuality are bad.

■ Relating Sexually

Your sexuality is deeply woven into who you are. And it affects the way you relate to other people. Because some

101

victims only receive affection when they are being abused, they learn to relate to men in a sexual way.

Remember the letter from Joanie? She said that the only time her father really paid attention to her or really talked to her was when he was abusing her sexually. Joanie should have been learning to talk to guys, have friendships with guys, eventually to have dating relationships, and someday to develop true intimacy with a man. Instead, her abuse taught her that sex was the only way to receive the attention and affection she needed and that every child needs.

Victims don't adopt these negative patterns of relating sexually on purpose. We don't even know we're doing it. Even if we come to recognize our actions, we don't know how to stop.

Remember my destructive, manipulative relationships with men? I realized I was using men, but I couldn't stop. I didn't know the truth about why I used men. Consciously, I felt terrible because I didn't want to be cruel. But what I didn't understand was that being cruel to men satisfied my subconscious need to be in control and act out my hatred for men.

> *Are you controlling and manipulating your relation-ships in order to maintain control of your life?*

■ Promiscuity

Sexual abuse victims have a history of misunderstanding and misusing sexuality. The effects of abuse have taught them deep-rooted lies. The underlying attitude of "Why not? I'm already used anyway. No good person will ever love me, so who cares?" leads many victims into promiscuity.

An abuse survivor often finds that sexual affairs provide a way—at least temporarily—to feel in control. Being sexually active allows her a "safe" way to express her contempt for men and their weakness in the face of her sexual power. Many victims are aware that they have a "strange power" in their bodies they can use to manipulate men. And most of them learn to use it.

Some victims are unable to maintain long-term sexual relationships. For a victim who experienced incestuous abuse, often the closer she gets to another person, the more "related" she becomes to that person. That makes it harder for her to experience any physical pleasure. After all, the person who first hurt her was "related," and that whole experience was linked to pain and shame.

Promiscuity in abuse victims often has little to do with sexual desire or even with sexual pleasure. Some victims involve themselves in sexual activity in hopes that they'll find "a knight in shining armor" who can undo the hurt of the past and protect them from future hurts. Others use sex as a way to feel "close" when they're desperately lonely. Sex seems to be the only way they know to bridge the distance they feel between themselves and others.

■ Lesbianism

Some girls who are sexually abused end up pursuing lesbian relationships. When we talk about what sexuality was really meant to be, you'll see that a sexual relationship with someone of the same sex is not good for you—not any more than casual sex is. But sometimes a young person who has been abused has trouble trusting and developing relationships with people of the opposite sex.

When I met Heather, she was seventeen. She dressed beautifully and kept her auburn hair short and trimmed to perfection. But she used to bite her nails down to the skin, and she often seemed nervous. I remember how startled I was the first time I noticed that Heather had dimples. I knew her a long time before I ever saw her smile.

When Heather was eight, her parents sent her to spend the summer with her grandma. Her eighty-year-old step-grandfather abused her all summer. He had a pacemaker, and she was terrified that anything she did to upset him would kill him. She could never confront him, and she couldn't bring herself to add to her grandma's troubles by telling her. So Heather confided the secret to the teenaged girl who came in to clean her grandmother's house. The girl told Heather that the old man had abused her, too. Heather developed a close relationship with the older girl who shared her secret. They began to have a sexual affair. Heather didn't want to be a lesbian, but she was afraid she was.

In the group setting, Heather was never able to talk about her relationship with the young woman who cleaned her grandmother's house. The other girls seemed "boy-crazy" to her. She wanted to remain a part of the group because she felt that the girls loved and accepted her, but she didn't think that girls who were struggling with heterosexual relationships would understand how she felt. So Heather worked through her sexual identity issue with a private therapist.

Through counseling, Heather discovered that the relationship initiated by the older girl was actually a second episode of sexual abuse perpetrated against her. Again

Heather had been involved in sexual contact that she hadn't freely chosen. Heather realized that her fear that she was a lesbian was just another lie her abuse experiences had told her. It was awhile before Heather could pass the big roadblock of forgiving both of her abusers, but she did it.

Then Heather began to date. Every time a "storm" came up in any relationship, she tended to blame it on her history of lesbianism. But eventually she realized that the girls around her were sharing similar stories about their relationships. Now Heather knows that a "stormy" teenage relationship is normal.

■ Is Sex Bad?

One of the lies abuse teaches victims is that "Sex is bad," and so any sexual feelings you have are bad, and that you are bad for having those feelings. Sex as it was created to be is *not* bad. As a matter of fact, we're going to devote a whole chapter to just how beautiful and wonderful sex really is!

Sexual feelings are not bad, but it's no wonder sexual abuse victims *think* they are. The early abuse brings up sexual feelings the victim never knew she had, ones she never asked to feel in the first place, ones she wishes would go away.

You're not bad because you have sexual feelings. You were created as a sexual being. You need to remind yourself that your abuse has nothing to do with what sex was intended to be and that *the guilt and shame belong always and only to the actions of the abuser, not to sex or your sexuality.*

It's important that you learn the truth about sex and sexuality because if you feel bad about who you are sexually, you will feel that you are "bad to the core." That feeling of shame about who you are will affect all of your actions and relationships—especially when you meet that one someone you'll love and trust enough to share the rest of your life with. And that's why we've devoted a whole chapter of this book to "The Wonderful Truth about Sex."

15

The Great Escape

ALL OF US WHO HAVE BEEN ABUSED HAVE TRIED OUR own methods of "escaping," even though we may not realize that our thoughts and actions are actually emotional or physical attempts to avoid abuse.

Maybe you'll recognize some of these types of "escape."

■ Imagination/Denial

When I was being molested by my neighbor, I talked to the Cocker Spaniel about being dead. Well, "being dead" was my way of escaping what was being done to my body and my mind.

I know of a girl named Cindy who "became" a blue couch whenever her uncle abused her. In her mind she just came out of her body and went into the couch. Then her uncle really couldn't hurt her because she wasn't there.

"Being" dead or "becoming" a blue couch are means of emotional survival—the abuse victim just couldn't live through it any other way. This type of escape is useful to the victim while the abuse is happening, but if the abuse issues aren't dealt with, the submerged pain will always find a way to come out.

■ Making Yourself Unattractive

After I was raped, I cut my hair off and refused to wear make-up. I hoped it would make me unattractive to men so they would leave me alone. Some victims overeat and become obese for the same reason. Others skip taking baths or never brush their teeth—anything to make them "ugly" enough to be safe.

Sometimes aggressive and hostile behaviors like physical fighting or mouthing off with obscenities become a defense against abuse for the same reason: the victim hopes that she will be too aggressive to be "attractive" to an abuser.

What these abuse survivors are not realizing—what I didn't realize—is that *nothing about them asked for abuse*. Sexual abuse happens because something is very wrong with the abuser, not because the victim is irresistible.

■ Drugs and Alcohol

Too often abuse survivors turn to drugs and alcohol, hoping to dull the pain or erase the memories. Did you know that 70 percent of teenage drug abusers have experienced family sexual abuse? But instead of escaping, abusers of drugs and alcohol are actually adding another bondage to their lives.

■ Running Away

It isn't unusual for sexual abuse victims to run away in an attempt to escape their abuse. Remember Mary? She ran away five times, and each time she was brought back because she never told anyone why she was running away.

I know one girl who ran away and was brought back by the police so many times that she would actually run away straight to the police station! She knew they would find her anyway, and she was resigned to having to go back, but it was a temporary safe place and a reprieve from home. The officers got to know her and allowed her to stay until the evening shift went off duty.

Even as an adult, I found ways to "run away." After my rape, I stayed with various friends and even changed jobs and moved to a new place where nobody would know about my past.

But running away never solves anything, because the painful memories and shame go with the abuse victim wherever she goes.

In what ways have you attempted to "run away"?

■ Marriage

Too many incest victims use marriage as an escape. But because a victim feels she is "bad," she will often marry a man who gives her the poor treatment she thinks she deserves. Often she will choose a man who is an emotional or physical abuser, or who abuses drugs and alcohol. Many times she will marry a man who will abuse their children.

I worked with a lady named Elsa who was thirty-three years old and had already been married six times! Elsa might as well have married the same guy every time, since each husband abused her. Because of the shame she felt from the abuse she had suffered as a young girl, she believed—subconsciously—that abuse was what she deserved. A guy didn't seem like the right "fit" unless he hurt her. Marriage was never meant to be an escape from sexual abuse, so of course it doesn't work as one. You don't leave your bag of garbage at the altar. You take it with you into the marriage, and it will affect your relationship—especially sexually—with your husband.

One woman told me, "I feel like I want to hide from God when I'm having sex with my husband." She was sure surprised when I told her that when God saw her making love with her husband, he probably said, "Well done, good and faithful servant!"

Husbands and wives are supposed to express their love and intimacy through sexual union. But when you marry to escape abuse, you don't know the truth about love and sex. You don't know the difference between abuse and making love.

So marriage isn't the answer. But there is hope. These patterns of abuse-looking-for-abuse can be broken. How? *By learning the truth about what love and sex are meant to be and how they are to come together in marriage.* We'll be looking at those truths in later chapters.

■ Suicide

There was a time in my life when I could no longer live with who I thought I was—and I reached for a knife. Suicide seemed to be the only way out—the "ultimate escape."

Do you feel that kind of despair? Are you tired of trying to cope with the pain and memories of your abuse? Do you feel angry and confused by the hopeful and happy people you go to school with? Then you know how I felt; you understand how suicide starts to look like a good option.

We'll never know how many teenage suicides are the result of sexual abuse. I only hear the stories of those who survive their attempts—like Jenny:

> For the first sixteen years of my life, I simply let it happen. I didn't even know what "it" was. But I knew the result of "it" was pain, deep emotional pain that led me to think about suicide constantly.
>
> I woke up in the emergency room of a hospital hating the fact that I was still alive. I had taken a massive overdose; I should have died. At the time when the doctors had anticipated that I would die, a strange thing happened. Life flowed through my veins, and the poison of the overdose did nothing. And was I ever mad! Finally, I'd hoped to die to the pain I'd been experiencing. Slowly the story unfolded, and what I remembered led me to three psychiatric hospitals and several suicide attempts.

Jenny is one of the fortunate ones. She *lived*. She dealt with her abuse issues. I'll never forget the happiness in her voice the night she called to tell me she was engaged to a man who not only knew about her past but was already meeting with her counselor. It would have been one of the worst things in the world for Jenny and her boyfriend to pretend that "it" (her abuse and her suicide attempts) didn't matter, that "it" was all over so they could just go on with life. Through counseling they learned that there are

111

events in life that trigger difficulty in a lot of abuse victims—such as things your husband might do that remind you of your abuser or when your children become the age you were when you were abused. Now Jenny will recognize what's happening and be ready to get whatever help she needs when those events occur.

An Important Message

If you often think about committing suicide, please find someone you can trust and talk to him or her. If you don't feel that anyone you know can understand or help you, go to your school counselors, family physician, minister, priest, or rabbi, or look in the Yellow Pages under "suicide" for a local crisis hotline or family service agency. There is no problem so big that suicide is the solution.

■ How Do You Escape?

Maybe you've tried to escape; maybe you're still trying. Maybe this is the first time you've been aware of the reasons why you overeat or don't take care of your body.

Imagination, making yourself unattractive, running away, drugs and alcohol, and suicide are not the answers. The only effective way to escape abuse and the pain you're living in is to learn the truth and replace the lies your abuse taught you with the truth. The truth is what will help you get beyond your sexual abuse into the light of loving, trusting relationships. And the first step in seeking the truth is seeking help.

16

Life at Home

FOR SEX ABUSE SURVIVORS, LIFE AT HOME CAN BE REALLY hard for lots of different reasons.

If you were abused by someone outside your family and are trying to keep what happened to you a secret, then you have a tough job. It's hard to keep such a secret from the people who know you best. The abuse-related emotions and actions we've been talking about may be causing problems: lots of arguments with your parents or brothers and sisters, withdrawal from your family, or new habits of obscene or hostile "leave me alone" attitudes. All of these emotions and actions put you under a lot of serious stress that's bound to affect your relationships at home.

Maybe your grades at school have slipped, and your parents are freaking out. It could be that you've slipped into a "self-destruct" mode because you feel so much shame.

Sometimes the actions that follow abuse can be the type that get you into trouble at school.

If you're being abused by someone inside your family, you might be using all your energy trying to prevent the abuse from happening again. If you are being abused by your father or step-father, or perhaps your mother's live-in boyfriend, you may be part of what is called "the incest triangle."

■ The Incest Triangle

The incest triangle is often the result when a woman who has been sexually abused marries a man who meets her "need" to be punished. (About 75 percent of girls I've talked with who are involved in father—or step-father—to daughter incest have mothers who were also sexually abused. Some of these mothers didn't remember their own abuse until the daughters disclosed what was happening and began treatment.) Because of the mother's continuing guilt feelings and shame, she often chooses an immature man who abuses drugs, alcohol, herself and, eventually, the children.

Since the mother hasn't dealt with her abuse, she falls into patterns that contribute to the abuse of her daughter. When the daughter reaches the age when the mother was molested, the mom often pulls away from the girl, leaving the daughter confused, adding to her feelings of guilt and shame. The mother also tends to pull back from her husband who is probably around the age of the man who abused her when she was a child. This withdrawal makes the father feel isolated, lonely, and often angry.

As the mother withdraws, the daughter may begin caring for the house and any other children—in a sense she "replaces" her mother. Because the mother is distant, the father and daughter naturally draw closer emotionally, trying to understand the mother's withdrawal. All too often this alliance leads to sexual involvement between the father and daughter.

■ Fathers and Daughters

An abusive father is often extremely "over-protective" or jealous of the child he's been abusing, sharply restricting her contact with her peers because he is afraid she will tell someone what happens at home. She may not be allowed to date because her abusive father has a competitive fear that his daughter will choose her date over him.

The abusive father may pay special attention to the daughter he's molesting—more than she ever wanted. One victim's father brought her flowers or candy every week. He treated her like a date, confusing her even more. She felt guilty when she wouldn't accept his gifts and angry when she did.

■ Mothers and Daughters

Often a mother who hasn't worked out her own issues about abuse will treat her daughter almost as a rival. I know one mother who actually told her daughter that if the daughter's teenaged boyfriend ever got into bed with her (the mother), he would never want to see the daughter again.

Sometimes a mother may dress like a teen or pay too much of the wrong kind of attention to the guys her daughter brings home. Many girls have told me they feel afraid or embarrassed to bring boyfriends home because their moms flirted with the boys.

When one mother was called by hospital staff who told her that her daughter had been sexually abused, she arrived at the hospital in short shorts and a tight t-shirt. "Sorry it took me so long," she said. "I had to change. Isn't this the cutest little outfit? My daughter just got it for her birthday, and I couldn't wait to wear it!" This mother's attitude was completely inappropriate at *any* time, much less at a time when her daughter needed her love and support.

These mothers seem to be trying, in a sad way, to regain the normal adolescence that was stolen from them as a result of their own abuse.

It isn't unusual for a mom to deny that her daughter is being abused. Remember Tonya, the girl who went to live with her grandmother because her mother didn't believe her story of abuse?

If the mother has been abused herself, it's often too painful or frightening to admit and deal with her daughter's abuse because of the personal memories or feelings it drags up.

Some mothers who admit the abuse even accuse the girls of causing it to happen. Remember that when Kim's sister, Kay, told her mom about her abuse, her mom told her it was *her* fault for acting sexy and not staying away from her father. My step-mother told me her father abused me because I was always sitting on his lap and hugging his neck. But remember, the responsibility for the abuse lies *always and only with the abuser,* no matter what you're told.

Unfortunately, mothers who struggle with insecurity and issues of self-worth and fear often can't face the prospect of life without their husbands or live-in boyfriends. This kind of mother ignores the victim's cries for help. In many cases, instead of protecting her daughter, the mother will even punish her for telling the truth. Some mothers blame their daughters for the financial problems their families face when the perpetrators are removed from the home.

> *Do you feel like your mom has betrayed you by not believing you?*

Even moms who haven't been abused often have a lot of trouble acknowledging and dealing with the fact that their husbands are injuring their children.

After talking about incest on a television program, I received this letter from an honest mom named Jeannie:

Dear Jan—

I have a different view on sexual molestation—my view as the mother of a victim.

It seems like a horror that will never go away. I sensed that all was not well with my husband (the victim's father), but I never guessed or even thought about sexual abuse until one night my five-

year-old, an only child, told me graphically what
she did with Daddy. My world slammed to a
screeching halt—along with my heart.

I reported him. . . . He was indicted (it took two
minutes). My daughter was put in counseling. . . .
He was convicted in a trial recently and given
probation with treatment.

Now you may think I'm crazy or sick, but as I
live and breathe, I tell you the truth: I still have
feelings for the man . . .

Jeannie loves her husband and her child; she is caught
smack dab in between. Don't condemn Jeannie—she is a
courageous and truthful mother. She is honest about her
feelings, yet she acted responsibly for the good of her child.
She believed her little girl and did all that was necessary
to protect her.

■ Brothers and Sisters

> *Do you feel rejected by your brothers and sisters?*

When an abusive parent pays special attention to one child,
the brothers and sisters often resent her special standing,
adding to her loneliness.

Being rejected by brothers and sisters is especially hard
for an abuse victim who is allowing her own abuse to
continue because she's been told by her abuser that if she
cooperates with him, he won't do the same thing to her
brothers and sisters. The sad truth is that a perpetrator is
often abusing several or all of the children in the family. He

counts on each child's desire to protect the others to keep his secret safe. So don't keep quiet, hoping that your brothers and sisters won't be abused if you don't tell. Abusers aren't honest.

Sometimes knowing about the abuse of another sibling can cause even more guilt and shame than your own abuse. Shelly wouldn't look at me as we talked about the possibility that her father had abused her sister.

"I hate myself," she finally confessed. "I knew all along that he was abusing her but I didn't do anything about it. But it's even worse—I knew, and I was glad. I was glad because it meant he wouldn't come to my bed that night!"

Shelly felt an overwhelming sense of shame that she had purchased a night's relief at the expense of her sister. It took a long time for Shelly to believe the truth—that her father was a sick man who would have abused her sister no matter how many times he abused Shelly.

■ Not Exactly the Cosby Show!

Obviously, life at home for victims of sexual abuse can be a far cry from the happy-go-lucky, free-and-easy families we sometimes see on TV. Many go home to deep and complicated family problems.

It's hard enough to deal with the effects of sexual abuse without feeling as if you carry the responsibility of what happens to your entire family. I know it may be difficult for you to believe, but that is not your personal responsibility! The blame for the problems in your family belongs *always and only* to the abuser. No matter what circumstances existed that may have made it easy for him to abuse, he made the choice.

119

And I understand that doesn't stop you from wishing you could do something to help your brothers and sisters—and even your mom and dad. One thing you *can* do is share the truths you're learning and the changes those truths allow you to make in your life with your family. If you've started, or are ready to start, your own journey through the effects of your abuse, you need to understand that you can't force your family to go with you. That choice is up to them. You can only decide to go yourself.

17

Especially for Guys

IN SOME WAYS I FEEL UNCOMFORTABLE WRITING ABOUT the specific effects and problems that boys and young men experience after sexual abuse. After all, I was abused as a girl and a woman and never as a boy! Personally, I've never grappled with the special issues abused guys deal with. What I've learned is from studying and from talking with boys and men who have been abused.

So here goes . . .

■ Alone with the Problem

All abuse victims feel alone with the memories and effects of their abuse. But it's worse than usual for guys. Our society has certain attitudes about masculinity (guys have to be tough) and male victimization (you must be a wimp) that tend to alienate guy victims even more than girl

121

victims. For instance, it's O.K. for a *girl* to need help and to seek help for the problems resulting from abuse, but it's not O.K. for a guy. People think he shouldn't need help when he is hurt. Instead, he should "take it like a man."

And because of these views, even though sexual abuse against girls is grossly under-reported, even fewer guys report being abused. Yet current estimates show that *one in four* guys has been sexually abused by his senior year of high school.

Statistics also indicate that guys are more likely than girls to be abused by someone outside the family. Very often they come from single-parent families, and they are often physically abused as well as sexually abused.

■ Sexual Identity

Guys experience the same struggles with fear, guilt, hatred, bitterness, and shame that sexually abused girls experience. But because they are most often abused by a member of their same sex (90 percent of all sex abusers are male), they are also confronted with the issue of sexual identity.

Sometimes a boy who was sexually assaulted by a man will start to wonder if there is something about him that said "homosexual" and his abuser could tell. Of course, this isn't any more true than a girl's fear that she was at fault because she was "sexy." But again, fears resulting from sexual abuse are not rational. And because of that, I can't repeat this often enough: *the responsibility and blame for any circumstance of sexual abuse belongs always and only to the abuser and never to the victim.*

Other guys who have been abused by men are afraid that the abuse experience has automatically made them homosexual, or else they are afraid that if they make the abuse known they will be labeled "homosexuals."

> *The reason for the abuse always lies with the abuser's perversions and problems and never with the victim.*

Violent acts—even sexual ones—committed against you have nothing to do with the real, true, inside you that God intended you to be. Someone's putrid actions against your body cannot make you someone you are not. Unfortunately, it's easy to swallow these lies along with all the other lies that sexual abuse feeds its victims. Guys who have suffered sexual abuse worry or wonder if they are homosexual.

■ Jack's Story

When Jack was thirteen, he was really scrawny. His hormones for growing hadn't really kicked in yet, and people always thought he was younger than he was—which he hated, of course. Right before Jack started the eighth grade, he went on an end-of-the-summer hiking and fishing trip with his uncle John. On the last night of their trip, Uncle John abused Jack sexually.

Uncle John was his mom's favorite little brother, so Jack never told anyone. But he refused ever to go camping with Uncle John again.

When school started, Jack tried to get into classwork and other activities and forget what had happened. In Environmental Science, he was assigned a girl named Becky as a lab partner. Becky had long, shiny hair, and she always smelled great. Jack thought she was really cool, but even though she was perfectly nice, he could never find anything to talk about with her. Jack asked a friend named Wendy to the first dance of the school year, but she turned him down because she already had a date with another guy. Jack had used up all his nerve asking her, so he didn't try to get another date.

Not long after, Jack began to experience the feelings of sexual desire that are quite normal for a guy his age. He found himself thinking about sexual things more often, and he noticed that he was easily stimulated visually. Jack also discovered that he sometimes felt excitement around guys as well as girls. Although this was also normal, Jack wondered if his sexual feelings were a result of his recent experience with his uncle.

Jack was starting to wonder about himself. *I'm no good with girls,* he thought, *and now I'm having feelings I don't even want to have. Maybe Uncle John knew something about me that I didn't even know. Maybe I am gay.*

■ So What's Normal?

Sexual identity is a tough issue for guys who have survived abuse. Guys reach their sexual-performance peak sometime around seventeen to nineteen years of age. So, for teen guys, the sexual drive is very intense. For guys, sexual feelings are localized in the genitals, which results in a sexual orientation to seek direct discharge. That's not bad or wrong—that's the way guys are made! (A girl's sexual orientation is different. And that's not bad or wrong either—that's just the way girls are made.)

Guys are also more visually stimulated than girls. That means when they see another person—a girl or a guy—they feel sexual excitement just from looking. Especially in the teen years, *it's very normal for guys to feel sexual excitement quite easily.* And guys have to learn to live with all the hormones that are going crazy in their bodies.

But guys who have been abused worry that they are homosexuals because they feel this sexual excitement sometimes when seeing or even visualizing a person of the same sex. These feelings are not abnormal for *any* guy, but the sexual abuse victim remembers his experience of sexual abuse and associates the abuse by a same-sex abuser with these normal feelings (another of the lies of sexual abuse).

> *Are you afraid you're a homosexual because girls don't "turn you on"?*

Another normal feeling for teenage guys is frustration in dating relationships with girls. Stormy teen relationships are normal, and feelings of inadequacy with girls are practically universal. These feelings come to all guys and girls in their teen years because of all the changes in life, in responsibility, and especially in body. For one thing, all teens are becoming men and women *physically* faster than they are becoming adults *emotionally* or *psychologically*. It's a tough time for everybody—even those people who look like they have their act together. These feelings of confusion or inadequacy don't mean that a guy will never have a successful intimate relationship with a girl; they don't mean that a guy will always feel inadequate around girls. And these feelings DO NOT mean that a guy is a homosexual.

Another normal aspect of your years in junior and senior high is that you make close friendships and develop a sense of camaraderie with people of your same sex. Until puberty, there weren't so many differences between the two sexes. But once the male and female differences really start to show up, you start hanging out and feeling more comfortable with people who are experiencing the same changes you are experiencing. It's normal to want close friends of your same sex. But for abused guys, whose experience with a same-sex abuser is twisting the truth, these new and normal same-sex friendships can be really scary. They get nervous that these feelings of closeness mean they are homosexuals. It's even worse if they've had a couple of rotten experiences with girls (which most teen guys do have!). They start to think, *I feel safe with guys, and girls reject me—so there must be something wrong with me!*

Another problem is that the way guys' sexual functions work, it's very easy for them to experience feelings of sexual pleasure during their abuse. Just as a person can't help sneezing if someone tickles his nose with a feather, a guy can't help being sexually aroused when stimulated in certain ways. *Experiencing an erection or orgasm during sexual abuse does* not *mean that you have homosexual tendencies!* It also doesn't mean that a guy "wanted" to be abused or that he was giving his abuser any kind of "permission" to make sexual contact.

■ Abused by a Woman

Guys who were sexually abused by women also face tough struggles. They may feel wimpy because our culture usually places men in the role of sexual aggressor, and they had that role taken away from them. They may also feel terrible because their abuse was shameful and painful instead of pleasurable and exciting. *What's wrong with me?* they might think. *As a red-blooded guy I'm supposed to enjoy this!* In a real-love relationship, a woman is loving and nurturing in sexual contact, not exploitative. Many guys who have experienced abuse by a woman keep a distorted image of women and the sexual relationship that carries into their adult lives and into their marriages.

One of the most difficult of all abuses to overcome is when mothers abuse their sons. The person who was most to be trusted, the one a son counted on to love and protect him, was instead most untrustworthy and destructive. The anger and hatred that typically result from this type of abuse is terrible. Victims of this type of abuser are often violent in their actions against women.

■ Displacing the Hurt

When girls are abused, they tend to victimize themselves. Girls tend to go out into life after abuse feeling that they deserved what they got. The result? Many times they land in still more abusive situations.

Some guys react the same way. But most guy victims of sexual abuse tend to victimize others, acting out their anger and hurt in ways that damage others.

Obviously, there are better ways of dealing with the pain of sexual abuse than to victimize yourself or others, but it must be *your choice* to get help.

■ Getting Help

Because of all the reasons we talked about, it is especially hard for guys to come forward and get help when they've been abused. But it's important and necessary. A friend of mine offers this advice especially for male victims:

> So much of the past enters into the people we are today. But as I grow and mature, I am striving to learn how to be a *real* man. Part of the process of shaping my character was to weed out my past by talking with people I know and respect. There is nothing like the cleansing feeling I experienced after learning how to deal with and overcome my past. I strongly encourage all young men to seek help.

The man who wrote this message is not a coward or a wimp. He is not a cowering weakling without any masculinity. He's Mike Singletary, the all-pro middle linebacker for the Chicago Bears. And if you've ever seen Mike play football, you know he's no coward or weakling! Mike is a "real" man, yet he admits that he needed help in dealing with the past. Mike knows that being a real man means much, much more than putting on a uniform and tackling gigantic opponents. It takes more courage to deal with the problems of the past than it does to risk being flattened by a 240-pound football player.

■ The Promises Are True!

Because I know the pain of sexual abuse, I can understand at least a little of what guy victims are suffering. But the promises of God are true for every guy as much as they are for a female victim. The real, true inside man can be free from the lies of the past. The garbage can be dumped to reveal a healthy, happy man who can experience the celebration of real love with a woman.

I believe that with all my heart because I've seen it happen. And it can happen for you, too.

Getting Together, Learning the Truth

18

Support Groups

I'VE MENTIONED SUPPORT GROUPS SEVERAL TIMES IN this book. Now it's time for you to find out exactly what a support group is and what it has to offer you.

Support groups are made up of teens like yourself and a leader. All the group members will have experienced some form of sexual abuse, either earlier as a child, more recently as a teen, or, in some cases, both. The purpose of the group is to help victims identify the emotions, hurts, and difficulties in their lives because of the abuse. The group members learn to draw support, understanding, and encouragement from each other to help deal with the results of being sexually abused. Members help each other see the lies in their lives and replace those lies with freeing truth. They really make the journey much easier for each other.

Joining a group of sex abuse victims is scary. It takes a lot of guts just to show up because that means admitting to the others there that you are a victim. And it takes even more guts to tackle the issues and lies and obstacles in your journey through abuse and beyond into who you really are. But I think being part of a group is one of the most important things you can do for yourself.

Why? Because all the groups' members have been abused, you will feel understood and accepted right away. You'll quickly learn that you don't have to be afraid that talking about your experience will leave you open to blame, pity, rejetion, or shocked silence—reactions you may have experienced or been afraid you would experience if you told. A support group will give you, maybe for the first time, the kind of safety in sharing with others you've been waiting years for.

Most of the girls who attend my groups come because I spoke in their school or church. They heard me tell my story. They saw that I looked healthy and happy. Those who dare to hope meet with me one-on-one. At first they're suspicious—they want to know if I'm "for real." They ask questions and "feel me out" until they finally share their own stories.

■ Expectations

If you became a member of one of my groups, I'd expect five things from you. You'd find similar expectations in most groups. The first is that *you show up—on time—for group meetings.* The second is that *you know that you don't have to say anything if you don't want to but that anything you want to say is welcome.* The third thing is that *you share the goal of supporting the others in the group*—that means not saying things like, "That's dumb!" or "You should have known better!" in response to anyone's sharing. The fourth expectation is honesty; *you have to tell the truth about the emotions you're feeling and the things you struggle with.* And the fifth thing is probably the most important: *you have to promise never to share any information learned about the life of any group member with a person outside the group.* We abuse survivors know that the last thing we need is to have another trust betrayed.

At the first group meeting, we go over the rules and begin to get to know each other. I give everyone a list of *Topics for Group Discussion.* They take it home, mark the subjects they want to talk about, and bring it back to the next meeting. For the rest of the meetings, we talk about what the girls marked on their sheets.

Because support groups can be such an important part of your journey, I want you to "get the feel" for what it would be like to be in one. So I'm going to let you "sit in" on three meetings I led a few years ago. Although there's not as much give and take in these particular meetings as there usually is in our groups, I've picked these three because the girls and I were discussing what I feel are three important topics for sex abuse victims to learn the truth about: God, love, and sex.

You've already met the girls in this group: Sherry, Megan, Kim, Christy, Teresa, Tonya, and Heather. Try to picture yourself in these meetings. Notice how comfortable the girls are with one another, how free they are to voice their opinions and to disagree with each other and with me.

19

The Awesome Truth about God

"**I** WAS SURPRISED TO SEE THAT EVERY ONE OF YOU listed God as a topic you want to talk about," I began as soon as everyone was seated.

"Why?" asked Heather. "Did you think we never think about God? I mean, even if you don't believe he exists, everybody wonders sometimes if he does."

"No, it's not that I thought you never considered his existence. It's just that it's unusual for *everyone* in a group to recognize God as an issue in dealing with their sexual abuse," I replied.

"Well, I don't know about anybody else, but I think about God a lot," Teresa said. "I guess that I worry about what God must think of me and the things I've done. My family used to go to church, and I know God hates sin. And a lot of the things I've done are what everybody calls sin. So I can't help but think about God."

Several of the girls were nodding their heads in agreement.

"O.K., I'm more than happy to talk with you about God. Do you remember when I told you about the night I was going to kill myself? That night a friend who loved me sent someone to tell me that I needed to let him back into my life. He said I needed to let him help me through my abuse because he still loved me. Well, that friend was God. God is the only one who has a love big enough to cover all the hurt of sexual abuse.

"But don't be afraid that if you don't believe in him he won't help you, because he doesn't operate like that. He understands why you feel the way you do about him, and he isn't angry with you. No matter how angry you are with him, that never stops him from loving you."

Do you have trouble believing that God loves you even if you don't love him?

"Still, I'm not sure I'd ever want to risk making God mad," Tonya commented. "From what I've heard about him—he could zap me anytime he wants to."

"You're right. He can zap you—or me—anytime he wants to. But I just happen to know him well enough to know he isn't going to do that. He doesn't get mad at us for things like not understanding his love for us. He knows why we feel the way we do," I told her.

"Are you trying to tell me that it's O.K. with God for me to be mad at him?" Heather questioned, unbelievingly.

"I didn't say it was O.K. It's never O.K. with God that we believe lies rather than the truth. I said he isn't angry

138

with us—and he still loves us. He wants us to believe the truth because, like he said, the truth will set us free. When you believe the truth you don't have to be a slave to lies anymore. You've seen how that works. As we see and then believe the truth about our abuse, we become free from slavery to the lies we have been taught."

"Yeah, we can see that," Teresa spoke for the others, "but that's not the same as being mad at God. You're not supposed to be mad at God. You're supposed to love God."

"Don't you ever get mad at people you love?" I asked her.

"Sure, at *people*. But I'm not supposed to get mad at God."

"Right," I agreed. "That's how it's supposed to be, but give God a little credit. He knows what's happened to us. Even if you don't act angry or yell at him, he knows the feelings you have inside. And I promise you that as long as you're honest in what you're telling him, you can argue out your pain and betrayal and anger with God anytime!"

"How do you know?" Tonya pressed.

So I told them about how I had shouted at and argued with God about the death of my childhood.

"Man, that's hard to believe," Tonya said.

"What do you think—she's making it up?" Megan leaped to my defense.

"No, that's not what I mean. I just mean it's hard to believe."

"That's O.K., Tonya," I jumped in. "I know what you mean, and you're right. It *is* hard to believe, but it's true. Just like it was hard to believe but true that your abuse wasn't your fault."

Tonya shook her head slowly. "This is going to take awhile to sink in."

"It sure is," Teresa agreed.

"Hey, that's fair. This stuff is hard for people who haven't been abused to understand—much less people like us who have been hurt for so long. Most of us feel like it's only because God has bad aim that we haven't been struck by lightning long ago!"

The girls laughed, and a couple of them nodded.

"But it isn't. It's because he loves us," I assured them.

"Oh, yeah?" Megan challenged. "If he loves us so much, where was he when Teresa's cousin was raping her? Where was he when Sam raped me?"

None of the other girls spoke, but I knew they were all waiting to hear my answer. So I explained.

> *Do you ever wonder where God was when you were being abused?*

■ Looking Back

In order to see where God is coming from, we need to go back and look at some basic facts about God and the world.

When God created the world and the first human beings, Adam and Eve, he gave them free choice. That means they could decide whether or not they would do what God told them to do.

We're all given that same choice. The only difference is that before Adam and Eve ate the fruit from the tree of the knowledge of good and evil, they didn't even know evil existed. All they knew was that they weren't supposed to eat that fruit. And that was fine with them. They had plenty of other things to eat. They lived in the garden with each other and talked with God. Their world was good. They didn't know about evil.

But, you see, Satan wanted them to know about evil. Satan has hated God ever since he decided he wanted to be God and God wouldn't let him. So he talked Eve into disobeying God, and, from that day forward, everyone who has ever been born (we're all descendants of Adam and Eve) has known about evil and has had to choose between doing good or doing evil. That was what the devil wanted because he knew some people would choose to do evil and that would hurt God.

And that's exactly what happened when you were abused: someone chose to do wrong. Your abuser chose to put his desires above your rights as a human being. He chose to use you to fulfill his wants. That hurts you, and when you hurt, God hurts.

Now that I've come to understand a little about God's love for us, I believe that when you were being abused God was there, crying, just like he was there, crying, when they crucified his Son. Both were the result of people choosing wrong, and both caused pain to innocent people, so both hurt God.

■ Putting a Stop to It

"Hey," Tonya interjected, "if it hurts God so much when we're hurt, why doesn't he just put a stop to it instead of just crying? He's supposed to be so powerful—why doesn't he just zap the people who choose to do wrong? Or better yet, couldn't he just wipe everybody out and start all over again?"

"If he zaps everyone who chooses to do wrong, we wouldn't have free choice. Would you want to live like a programmed robot?" I asked her. "Think about it. You want the right to make choices, don't you?"

"Well, sure, but I would never *choose* to abuse anyone," Tonya insisted.

"I'm sure you wouldn't," I assured her. "But you have made wrong choices, haven't you? And sometimes your choices have hurt others. We've all made bad choices, and some of them have hurt other people. But would you really want God to take away free choice and make us all robots?

"As for wiping everybody out," I continued, "well, there was a time when people were making so many evil choices and hurting each other so much that God sent a great flood to drown all the people on the earth except Noah and his family. The first thing Noah did when his ark hit dry land was to build an altar and thank God for saving him. Sounds reasonable, doesn't it? But then he planted a vineyard, harvested the crop, made wine, and got drunk! Noah certainly made a bad choice that time!

"Now God knew that as long as there were people, they were going to make wrong choices. So what did God do about that? He made a choice. He chose to send his only Son, Jesus, to earth to die—to pay the price for the wrong and evil people do. God let his Son die to prove he loves us."

"Oh, I can believe God loves *you* now. You're doing good things now. But do you really think God loved you when you were—what did you call it?—'destroying the entire male population of the United States singlehandedly'?" Heather asked.

"No, I don't *think* God loved me when I was destroying men. I *know* God loved me then! And, more than that, I know he loved me just as much *then* as he does *now.*"

"How do you know that?" Teresa asked. So I told them this story.

■ A Different Kind of Love Story

About two years ago, I started working part-time with kids who had been sexually abused. For the first time in my life, I knew I was doing what I was meant to do.

About a year ago, I was attending a meeting for the corporation I worked for. One of the men I'd seen around but never talked with much made some comments during the meeting that caught my attention, and I was attracted to him. The night before we left the conference, he surprised me by telling me that he wanted me to get to be the best I could be, using whatever standard I measured myself by.

I just laughed and replied, "You might not want to say that, Norm, because my measuring rod is not this company."

"Oh, I know that—" he said, "You're a Christian. I know because I'm a Christian, too."

Now you'd think that knowing he was a Christian would have put my mind at ease. But it didn't. I was scared to death! He was the first man I'd been attracted to since I gave up hurting men.

In fact, I was so afraid of him that I went home and asked my most trusted friends to pray with me that he would disappear out of my life. I finally felt I had my life in order, and I didn't need any man messing it up for me.

But my friends wouldn't pray. They said they thought God had finally found someone who could handle me, and that wasn't easy—even for God!

As Norm and I began to get to know each other, I had to admit that Norm was exactly what I would have asked God for if I had thought I was good enough to deserve him (which I was sure I wasn't, so I hadn't asked).

143

> *Do you ever feel like you don't deserve a relationship*
> *with a "good" person?*

Norm is a truly amazing man, very sensitive and intuitive, but at the same time persistent and practical—about as unlike me as a person can get! He made me deal with a lot of the sexual abuse garbage I still had.

But the closer we got, the more afraid I became. I had moved to another state when I went to work for that company. No one knew "her," the part of me that treated men cruelly, that knew how to dress and walk to attract men, the part that knew exactly what men wanted to hear. Of course, when I started to do the programs in schools, everyone knew I had a past, but they really didn't know "her." They all thought I was a good person, but I wasn't so sure.

And the closer I got to Norm, the less sure I was. I wanted to have sex with him. I was horrified at the thoughts that kept popping into my head. They were the kind of things "she" did with men—and "she" wasn't supposed to be part of me anymore. But she was.

I was so scared that Norm would find out and say, "What in the world have I gotten myself into?" and I'd never see him again.

But that isn't what happened. I finally told Norm all about "her," the part of me that had lived so sinfully. And he didn't call me names or tell me to get out of his life. Instead he said, "Oh, Jan, you know better than to think you can hide anything from God. You need to give that part of you to God."

144

I promised that I would do it before I went to sleep that night. But when I tried, I just couldn't talk to God about all the shameful things I had done. I was afraid that if I called them to his attention, he would remember how horrible I really was. He couldn't love me if he remembered who I really was. I was sure he would take Norm away from me because deep, deep inside me, I was still evil.

I can't tell you how long I sat in the middle of my living-room floor and cried. I can't tell you how many times I told God I was sorry. But I couldn't tell him what I was sorry for because then he would remember what I was. The voices in my mind kept haunting me: "Did you really believe God was going to let you be happy with him? You know what you are! You'd have to be crazy to think someone like you could ever be someone like Norm wants! You're so stupid! You know you're not good enough for him! God loves him far too much ever to let him get involved with someone like you! What a fool!"

I felt as if big claws were tearing me apart inside. I believed that God had only accepted and loved me *because*, right then, I was being good. But I knew that I wasn't going to be able to keep on being good forever.

I've never felt as unlovable as I felt then—or as hopeless. I knew everything was going to fall apart around me. I could feel it. But since I had promised Norm, I knew I was going to have to talk to God. So I finally said, "She's still here, God. I can feel her sometimes when I talk to Norm. She's going to come out again. I know she is. She's hurt so many people. I know you're angry with her. I've tried. You know I've tried, but she's still here. You love me now because I'm being good. But she'll come back, and I'll be like I was before, and you can't love me anymore."

145

I sat there sobbing, waiting for God's anger to come down on me. But instead I heard a voice inside me say, "She's just a little child; she's hurt. She's been locked under a house in the dark with spider webs and bugs, afraid to move. She's been left alone in the dark in a closet. She's been violated in the dark by someone she trusted. She came out fighting for her very existence the only way she knew how. I've cried over her often, but I've never been angry with her. I've hurt for her because she couldn't let me love her, but I've never hated her. I love her—I always have—and I want you to love her, too."

"I can't," I argued, "You may never have been angry with the child, but there's no way you could ever love the woman she turned out to be."

"The woman lives with the child," the voice continued. "She feels the pain of the child. She behaves as she does to escape the pain. I've cried over her often, but I've never been angry with her. I've hurt for her because she wouldn't let me love her, but I've never hated her. I love her because she's part of you—and I love you."

In my entire life, I had never felt so loved or accepted. I knew that God loved me, and that I didn't have to be afraid of him. I no longer had to be afraid of "her" either—even though she had done lots of bad things because she had been abused. *God understood.* And he had sent his Son to pay for *everything* she had done. I didn't need to do more bad things to punish her because God had already forgiven her.

I couldn't love "her" that night—that didn't happen until I had worked through certain areas of my sexuality. But I didn't hate "her" anymore, and I was able to give "her" to God to love and protect until I was healed enough to accept and love "her" myself.

I learned something really important about God that night. You don't have to have your life all cleaned up before God will love you. He loves you even if you don't love him, even if you're angry with him. God loves you just like you are! But he also loves you so much that he won't leave you where you are. He wants to free you from all your past pain and guilt so that you can become all you're intended to be.

> *Can you believe that God understands you—and really loves you—just like you are?*

When I finished my story, there wasn't a dry eye in the group. *A mixture of happiness for me and hope for themselves,* I thought. So I was shocked when Tonya said, "See, I can believe God loves *you* like that. But I can't believe he loves me!"

"I guess I can understand that, because believing it sure didn't come easy for me either," I replied. "But I want you to think about what I'm going to say. I was forty-two years old before I began to deal with my abuse. So not only did I have the garbage the abusers had put into my bag, but I had been adding my own garbage for thirty-four years! That's at least twice as long as any of you have even been alive! If God can love *me* with all that accumulated garbage and filth, doesn't it make sense that he can love you? I mean, I'm bound to have more garbage than any of you just because I'm older than you are, and I've been putting it in longer. Can you see that?"

"I can see it, but I can't feel it," Teresa said. "Look—I drink, I do drugs. My cousin started having sex with me when I was eight years old, and I've been sleeping around

147

since I was eleven. I'm still doing those things. There isn't one reason in this world why God would love me."

"I don't agree with you about that," I argued. "God has a big reason for loving you—he created you in his image. You are worth everything to him. He allowed his Son to die in your place because he loves you and thinks you're valuable. And he doesn't quit loving you even when you're acting unlovable."

> *Do you ever feel like there's not one good reason in the world for God to love you?*

■ From Bad into Good

God will never quit loving us *no matter what*. But that's not the only wonderful thing that he does. God also takes those things we think make us such bad people and turns them into our greatest assets. For example, God took my ability to get men to trust me and turned it into the ability to encourage leaders in schools, churches, and organizations to support programs on sexual abuse.

God takes the things that should have destroyed our lives and makes them into his greatest work. He took my abuse and made it into the desire and motivation to establish programs so that you and others like you don't have to carry the effects of your abuse around with you and ruin your lives. And he gave me the added blessing of helping you get started in your healing.

So you see, not only does God love you even if there really isn't one good reason in the world why he should, but he also takes the reasons why you think he shouldn't love you and makes them into things you can love about yourself!

■ You Are God's Treasure

Try closing your eyes and imagining with me for a minute that God is sitting beside you. Talk with God in your imagination, just as if you were talking with a friend. Tell him up front why you think he doesn't love you. Tell him the truth. Say exactly what you feel. If you're angry, tell him. If you feel worthless, tell him.

> *If you were talking to God about why you think he doesn't love you, what would you say?*

What do you imagine God is saying to you? Do you imagine him telling you that he doesn't love you, that you're not good enough, that you're not important to him, or that he can't forgive the things you've done?

Well, let me tell you what God is *really* saying:

- I created your innermost being. I knit you together in your mother's womb. You are fearfully and wonderfully made.

- Even the hairs of your head are numbered.

- As high as the heavens are above the earth, so great is my love for you.

- Neither the present nor the future, nor any powers, neither height nor depth, nor anything else in all creation, will be able to separate you from my love.

- I have loved you with an everlasting love.

- As far as the east is from the west, so far have I removed your wrongs from you.

- I will remember your wrongs no more.

If you don't believe me, check it out for yourself in the Bible, where all these words of love came from (Psalm 139:13-14; Matthew 10:30; Psalm 103:11; Romans 8:38-39; Jeremiah 31:3; Psalm 103:12; Isaiah 43:25).

God thinks you're beautiful and valuable. Did you know that he made you to be his greatest treasure? God created the entire universe, but nothing in it was valuable enough to buy with the life of his only Son except us—you and me.

So the next time you think you're unworthy or unlovable, remember the value God puts on you and how much he loves you.

Can you begin to believe that God might really love you?

I know it's not easy to accept that God loves us and thinks we're important when we don't love ourselves and feel lower than a worm! But he does. I never would have gotten from where I was to where I am if that weren't true.

If you don't feel loved by God right away, don't be discouraged. God's love is true and firm and unchanging. He will always be there for you. And remember, even if you can't accept his love yet, God is not angry with you. He'll never stop loving you!

20

The Real Truth about Love

"I HAVE A FEELING THAT TODAY'S GOING TO BE AN interesting day for us," I told the girls. "We're going to be talking about love and relationships."

"You mean boys?" Teresa asked.

"Well, we're going to focus on love in dating relationships, but the principles of real love apply to relationships with all the people in our lives," I answered. "Our first order of business is to understand love—what it is and what it is not."

So I shared the real truth about what love is and is not.

■ Immature Love

I love Norm, but I didn't have *real* love for him the first time he talked with me or even the first times we went out together. There were many things about Norm that I

153

responded to, things I wanted in my life. He's interesting to talk to. He's compassionate and caring; he never condemns or judges. And—on top of all that—he's good-looking! But at the beginning I loved Norm *because*—because he has a clever mind, because he's good-looking, because he makes me feel good. But that was immature love.

Immature love says, "I love you *because* . . ."

Immature love also says, "I love you *if*—if you love me, if you meet my standards."

And many times immature love says, "I'll love you *as soon as*—as soon as you meet my needs, as soon as you love me first."

Immature love always has a *reason*. It's self-centered, based on what another person does for you.

Have you ever experienced immature love? Have you offered immature love to others?

■ Real Love

Where immature love depends on the person we love being what we desire in attitude and behavior, real love says, "I love you in spite of your long nose." "I love you even though you're moody." "I love you even when you forget my birthday." Real love says, "I love you just because you're you" or "I love you for no good reason at all." Real love doesn't need reasons.

Real love is a decision, a commitment. It isn't something you fall into—it's something you jump into! Or at least step into.

Something changed when I committed myself to Norm. The principles of real love began to grow in me when I made

154

the decision that I was going to love him unconditionally, that I was going to meet his needs, instead of letting my love depend on what he was or could do for me.

Real love is forever. It doesn't stop because "You don't make me feel good" or because "You stopped being physically attractive." I love Norm even when he makes me angry or he hurts my feelings—I'll love him even when he gets chubby and bald.

Real love is sacrificial. If you really love someone, you keep giving and giving whatever it takes to benefit the person you love. You don't count up the costs of loving but spend love freely for the sake of the one you love. Real love asks, "What can I do to help you?" "How can I help you be and feel better?" "How can I love you more?"

When you really love someone, you can only be happy if the one you love is happy. And while you are busy making the one you love happy, you'll become happy, too! That's the beauty of true love.

But it's important not to confuse real love with allowing another person to hurt you. Whenever a person causes you harm, he automatically harms himself. Abusing someone causes psychological and emotional damage to the abuser. So it's never loving to allow someone to hurt you.

Real love forgives and forgets. If you love someone unconditionally, you don't keep track of all the wrong or bad things he's ever done to you. When you love someone, you let him start over fresh without punishment or grudges. You never bring up old hurts—especially not to remind him that you forgave him for being so rotten!

Love is real only if there isn't anything it can't forgive!

Are you keeping a mental list of wrongs someone—maybe a sister, brother, or an ex-best friend—has done against you?

Real love allows freedom. If you really love someone, you give him the freedom to be himself without fear of ridicule or rejection. You will let him express his feelings and opinions.

Please understand that this doesn't mean that if your boyfriend says he wants to express himself by having sex with you then you are to allow him that "freedom." That isn't freedom at all; that's using you for immediate gratification.

If this situation comes up, explain the damage having sex would do to your relationship. If your boyfriend can't accept your decision, then allow him the freedom to leave the relationship. Remember, real love is sacrificial. If you really love someone, you won't remain in a relationship if that relationship harms the other person.

Real love allows freedom within loving limits.

We'll talk more about those limits in the chapter on sex. Right now, let's look at an important fact about the freedom real love allows.

When I speak in a school assembly or church, I invite anyone who has been abused to come talk with me one-on-one. Hearing about my experiences and my healing gives victims the freedom to talk with me about their own abuse. The freedom of talking with me gives them the freedom to come into a group and share their experiences and learn the truth. And the freedom that comes with learning the truth gives victims the freedom to work through their sexual abuse in their own way, at their own speed.

Freedom is important for everyone, but it is an *absolute necessity* for abuse victims. Only when we have freedom from the lies our abuse taught us can we become all we really are meant to be.

Real love sees and affirms the unique value of the one loved. Those unique and wonderful characteristics are not the reasons you love someone but opportunities for you and the one you love to celebrate. It's impossible to love someone with real love and not see at least some good things about that person. If you really love someone, you'll look for those things and speak up about them.

Real love is not afraid to lose. It's not afraid to lose because real love stays away from any kind of power struggle. When two people really love each other, they share things they wouldn't share with others. Knowing these private things about another person gives you a certain power over that person, but it shouldn't be an authoritative, controlling power. Real love would never use that power to hurt. Instead, the power that comes with real love is trustworthy, only wanting to serve the loved one in a healthy way.

Earlier in my life, having men love me gave me a certain power, and I used that power to hurt them. But now I'm very protective of the things Norm shares with me—the things that he tells me he doesn't share with other people. How you *don't* use the power that love gives you tells you a lot about how far you've come in your healing.

> *Did someone you love take advantage of that love and abuse you? Has a friend ever betrayed your love by telling others the private things you've shared?*

Real love is nothing to be ashamed of. Loving someone is the biggest compliment you can ever pay another person. And feeling loved makes you feel more valuable than anything else! Real love is the most wonderful gift you can give—don't ever be ashamed of giving it!

Real love always finds the hidden need. There is always pain or a lack of love inside any person who hurts you that causes him or her to hurt you. Loving someone means looking for that pain or need instead of thinking about what that person did to you. A psychologist named Alfred Adler once said, "All human failure is the result of a lack of love." If that's true—and I believe it is—then the people who hurt you do it because they don't know about real love—not because there's anything wrong with you.

■ A Lack of Love

"Wait a minute," Tonya blurted out. "If that's true, then you're saying that the people who abused us didn't know enough about love, aren't you?"

"Well, if love is what I've been saying it is, can you imagine anyone who has real love abusing someone?" I asked her.

"No," she admitted. "You couldn't really feel love and still deliberately hurt someone like that. But does that mean it's not their fault that they abused us?"

"No, it definitely does not!" I was quick to assure her. "Our abusers certainly didn't know real love, but they *did* know the difference between right and wrong, and they *chose* to do wrong. They are still responsible for their actions. It's just that their actions may have been different if they had known and experienced true love in their own lives. And it was that lack of love, not a defect in us, that caused them to abuse us."

"In a way, that makes me feel better—and in another way, it's really sad." Christy was struggling with the hope she felt in receiving reinforcement that her abuse wasn't her fault and in realizing that abusers are humans who need love, too.

"Boy, getting this love bit right is turning out to be real important," Tonya said. "And there's a whole lot more to it than I ever thought. But it's going to be worth it, right, Jan?"

"Every minute of it!" I promised. "It's the most important thing you can learn and accept, as far as I'm concerned. But it sure doesn't come easy.

"Deep down inside, we all want to be loved. We're just scared to death. To love and to be loved, we have to open up and admit we need others. And admitting we need someone is risky business—it gives another person at least a certain amount of control in our lives. We're afraid to love, because we were abused by someone who had control in our lives. So, here we are, afraid of the one thing we need and want most in our lives!

"Can any of you tell me someone in your lives who has given you that kind of love?" I asked.

"I know two people who really love me," Teresa said immediately.

"Great! Who are they?" I asked.

"My dad and you. I've always known that even if nobody else in the whole world loved me, my dad always would. And ever since I talked to you alone that first day, I've known that you understood what I felt and you've been where I am. I know you love me, and I know I'm safe with you. You and Dad . . . I'm safe with both of you, no matter what."

"This is the first place I've ever felt safe," Kim put in. "I don't believe everything you've told us. I want to, and I'm trying, but I can't. But it does feel good to know you love me just like I am."

"We can really be a bunch of —— sometimes. Thanks for putting up with us and not making us feel like garbage," Megan added.

"I know you all think I'm a little weird anyway, so I guess I can't damage my reputation much," Tonya laughed. "I just want to say that I love everyone in this group. Just knowing you all are here has meant so much to me. I know what Kim means. This is the safest place I've ever known."

I sat and watched as the girls cried and hugged each other and talked about feeling safe and loved, something many of them were experiencing for the first time in their lives.

> *Do you have someone in your life who you know loves you with real love? If so, please go to that person and tell him or her about your abuse. Let that person give you the real love you need to help heal the effects of your abuse.*

"Hey, you guys." Tonya waited until she had everyone's attention. "I'll bet I know where all of us can get some more love."

"Where?" Christy asked.

"From God!" Tonya exclaimed. "Doesn't this unconditional, forever, without being afraid stuff sound like what Jan said about God last week? And besides, he sure loves Jan, and we all know how weird she is. I'm about convinced that if he can love her, he can love me. I'm not a whole lot weirder than she is!"

"I'm better at being weird than you are. I've had a few more years of practice at it." I laughed. "But you can certainly get real love from God. Actually all real love has something of God in it. It has to because *God is love*. That makes him the original source of all love.

"So in order for you to have real love to give, you have to get it from God. Now, he may give it to you through another person, but he is the source, so it has to come from him."

■ Real Love

All real love comes from God. Check out 1 Corinthians chapter 13 in the Bible for the best definition of real love I've ever read. It says, "Love is patient, love is kind. It does not envy, it does not boast, it is not proud. It is not rude, it is not self-seeking, it is not easily angered, it keeps no record of wrongs. Love does not delight in evil but rejoices with the truth. It always protects, always trusts, always hopes, always perseveres."

Can you imagine spending the rest of your life married to someone who loves you like that? That's exactly what

God wants for us. He wants it for all his children, but I think he wants it especially for us because he knows how much love we need to cover the pain and betrayal that are the results of our abuse.

All our lives we've built up our fortresses, acted out roles, and played games. Love gives us the freedom to take down the walls, block by block, as we gain courage and trust, until finally we're free to show the people who love us who we really are. Love gives us freedom to stop acting out roles and be ourselves. Love gives us the freedom to fail and start over with a clean slate. We're going to make mistakes, but failure doesn't mean a thing when a relationship is built on real love. Love gives us the freedom to stop playing games and really live.

Love gives us freedom to really live.

"It sure sounds great," Teresa admitted. "But where are we going to find guys who love like this?"

"Yeah, none of the guys I know have a clue about anything you've said," Sherry added. "Are you sure there really are guys who understand this stuff?"

"I'll bet Norm does." Tonya looked at me. "Doesn't he, Jan?"

"Yes, he does. As a matter of fact, he helped me understand it."

"I knew it!" she shrieked. "You know, the more I get into this, the better I like it. Before this is over, I'm really going to believe that God loves me as much as he loves you." She laughed. "Then I'm going to ask him to send me a younger version of Norm, and I'm going to fall in love—"

"You don't fall in love," Teresa reminded her. "You have to jump."

"Oh, yeah. Well, I'm going to jump into love and be just as happy as Jan is!" Tonya punctuated her sentence with an emphatic nod.

The girls looked at her, laughing and shaking their heads.

"I'm sure you will," I assured her. "Just be sure you don't stop with being as happy as I am right now. Understand that getting where I am has been a process, and it won't stop here. I'll keep on growing, and I fully expect to keep getting happier. It'll be that way for all of you, too!"

Can you imagine yourself feeling truly loved? Do you believe this could happen to you?

■ It Takes Time

Can you picture yourself receiving real love? Are you beginning to feel like this could happen for you? Can you feel a little hope that there is a God and that he loves you and wants you to receive and give the kind of real love we've talked about?

Remember: it wasn't easy getting to where I am now. I had to work my way through the same issues you're dealing with. There were times when I almost quit. There were lots of times when I felt that I took one step forward and five backward! And there were times when I failed and had to pick up the pieces and start again.

It takes time to work through all the lies abuse taught us. It also takes time to learn to receive and give real love.

163

But you can't find a better way to spend your time because the pay-off is fantastic! Once you've grown into real love—and when you have it to give and are healthy enough to accept the necessity of real love in your romantic relationships—you are ready to establish the kind of relationships that lead to marriage. And it's only within marriage that love gives us one of its most beautiful freedoms, the freedom to experience love and sex together, as the wonderful celebration they were meant to be.

21

The Wonderful Truth about Sex

AS I WATCHED THE GIRLS COME INTO THE ROOM, I wondered how this meeting would progress. Since we were going to be talking about sex, I knew it would probably be pretty lively. As soon as everyone was seated, I jumped right in.

"Okay, it's time to deal with sex as it should be—without abuse connected with it. I understand that doesn't come easy for some of us. Those of us who are sexually active use sex as a way to feel wanted or loved, to gain power, or sometimes even to hurt. Others of us are so repulsed by the act that we literally get sick to our stomachs just thinking about it. *Good, healthy,* and *beautiful* are not words we'd naturally associate with sex! But they should be—because along with words like *breath-taking, fantastic,* and *awesome,* they are words that perfectly describe sex as it

165

was intended to be, not the perversion we learned from our abuse.

"So our first order of business is to find the truth about sex. Who started it? Why was it created in the first place? How is it supposed to fit into our lives? Fortunately for us, there is a record of how sex got started."

"There is?" Megan's voice reflected her surprise.

"Sure," I replied. "Genesis, the very first book of the Bible, tells us that God created the heavens and the earth. Then he created the first man and woman in his own likeness. What does that mean? In what ways did God create us to be like himself? Well, for one thing, he gave us a spirit. For another, he made us sexual beings.

"Did you know that God himself has the characteristics we usually think of as feminine as well as the characteristics we think of as masculine? In the Hebrew language—that's the language the Old Testament was written in—the word for Holy Spirit is feminine. And throughout the Bible, God and Jesus are referred to as Father and Son."

"Wow! This is going to be interesting!" Tonya laughed.

Teresa agreed. "I never heard anybody in my church talk about God and sex together. Come to think of it, I've never heard anybody in my church talk about sex at all!"

"Well, some people are afraid that talking about sex as a wonderful, exciting celebration of love and discussing the way God relates to us through sex may lead young people into sexual experimentation or promiscuity," I replied.

"That can't apply to us," Christy pointed out. "We already know about sex."

"But the bad part is that a lot of what we in this group know about sex isn't true," I told her. "For example, what happened to you isn't what God intended sex to be at all. That lie needs to be replaced with the truth so that you

166

have the freedom to experience what God intended you to experience.

"So let's talk about how sex came about . . ."

■ The Creation of Sex

After God created the first man, he looked at him and said it wasn't good for him to be alone. But when he looked at everything he had made, he couldn't find a mate for the man. So he caused the man to go to sleep, and he took part of the man's side and made a woman to be his mate. Then God brought the woman to the man and said, "For this reason a man will leave his father and mother and be united to his wife, and they will become one flesh."

Human beings "unite" and "become one flesh" through the act of sexual intercourse. So from the very creation of man and woman, God intended for them to have sex.

Why did God want Adam and Eve to have sex? Well, God did tell Adam and Eve to "multiply on the earth," to have babies. But why did God choose sexual intercourse as the means of having babies? Why wouldn't he (as my favorite alternative suggests) just let us exchange earwax on Q-tips? I know that sounds funny, but so is sexual intercourse, when you think about it!

God never does anything without a reason. And ever since he made man and woman, his reason for everything is to help them know him and understand how much he loves them.

When you love someone with real love, you want that person to have everything that's good. You want to give that person wonderful gifts. After all, that's the nature of real love. And God is real love. Since he knows that the best thing for us is to "be united" spiritually with him, he gave

167

us, the people he loves, a way to live "union" on the earth. He gave us the gift of sexuality—and he created sex. The intimacy of real married love and sexual union form a picture and a physical example of the unmeasurable pleasure of spiritual union with God.

When you love someone with real love—the kind we've been talking about—and when you love that person enough to have committed yourself in marriage to him, then you will always want the best for him. And it's very natural to want to express your love by uniting and becoming one in the wonderful celebration of love that physical oneness offers. That's the way God intended for it to be.

The Bible doesn't record the unspeakable joy the first two lovers must have felt when God brought the first woman to the first man, but I'd like to share my favorite fictional account of the very first time the very first lovers made love.

■ The Very First Lovemaking

Spontaneously, they flew into one another's arms. With joy, with shouts, with laughter, and with tears, they clung to one another in wild embrace, yet all the while the man continued to cry, "You are beautiful, more beautiful than archangels. And I love you, I love you."

"And I love you, too," she replied.

Laughing in quiet delirium and exulting in uninhibited joy, he released his embrace and held her high in his mighty arms, threw back his head, and bellowed to the heavens, "I love! I love! And love has been returned."

With the excitement of a child, he held her at arm's length and cried again, "Did you know?! Did you know that you were once in me? Hidden in me! Here! See! You—such a beautiful creature as you. In me—right here in my side. That's where you were. And did you know? You are made of me! We were separated. Now look at us. We are together again. You have returned to me!" He pulled her toward him. "Together! Forever!"

And his final words seemed to roll across creation: "There remains but one thing, the ultimate completion of all oneness. First you in me, now I in you!"

So it came about, there in the serene beauty of the garden of Eden, while the angels rejoiced, the ruler of earth and his counterpart became, once more, one flesh.

Now *that's* a celebration! Can you imagine being completely free to feel all the joy and wonder of discovering the amazing physical differences and to experience the delights God had provided for them when he created those differences?

> *Do you have trouble believing that sex could be wonderful?*

"Are you trying to tell me that *that's* what sex is supposed to be like?" Kim sounded as if I'd just told her the world is flat.

"I know that's hard for most of us to believe, considering how we've experienced sex. But God did create sex to be a celebration of love, an act of completion, a coming together in order to become whole. And when it's done God's way, it is just that! Sex was *never* intended to bring pain—physical, emotional, or spiritual."

169

"So what happened?" Tonya wanted to know.

"Turning God's plans upside-down is Satan's territory. Ever since Satan wanted to be God and God wouldn't let him, he has hated God and has made hurting God his ultimate goal. So how does Satan hurt God? I mean, he can't hit God with a stick or kick him in the shins. The only way to hurt God is to hurt the people God loves—you and me. And he hurts us by trying to keep us from understanding and loving God. The best way to do that is to try to destroy God's perfect picture of 'oneness' so that we will never understand what it is to be one with God.

"And Satan has done a good job of perverting the natural desire for union that God placed in his creation. Those of us who have been hurt by people who gave in to Satan's perversion can certainly testify to that!"

"Yeah, it's really messed up sex for us," Sherry lamented.

"Oh, but it can be put back to what God intended for us," I assured her.

"Do you mean that even though I've been having sex with lots of guys for the last two years, it can be like this for me?" she questioned unbelievingly.

"Sure it can," I told her. "Not only can it be, but God wants it to be that way. He doesn't want you to live in the lies abuse taught you. He doesn't want you robbed of the wonder he intended sex to be. God loves you! And he wants you to have all the blessings he's prepared for you—and a good, healthy sexual relationship is one of his blessings."

Do you believe that God truly wants you to have a good, healthy sexual relationship?

"So how do we get from here—where we are—to there?" Tonya wanted to know.

"The first step is to understand the rules that God has set in place for physical union. Remember, the Bible said, 'For this reason a man will leave his father and mother and *be united to his wife,* and they will become one flesh.'

"Notice that, according to God's rules, a man was to be united to *his wife,* not to anyone who happened to be around when he got the urge, not even to anyone he thought he was in love with. He was to be united to his *wife only.* I know it's a short list, but you really get into trouble adding to it."

"Well that sure screws it up for us!" Megan spit the words from between clenched teeth.

"No it doesn't," I countered almost before she finished her sentence. "God knows that your sexual abuse was not your fault, was *never* your fault."

"Well he may not blame us for being abused. He's supposed to be fair," Teresa interjected. "But all of my sex hasn't been abuse. I was out looking for boys to have sex with when I was twelve years old."

"But Teresa, God knows you made a lot of choices that were influenced by your abuse. He just wants you to agree with him that sex outside of marriage is wrong and that you want to leave it behind with all the other lies and effects of your abuse. Then God will forget all about it!"

"Are you trying to tell me that all I have to do is agree that I was wrong and say I'm sorry, and then God will just act like it never happened?" Theresa's unbelief was evident in her voice.

"That's right."

"How do you know?" she questioned.

"In the Bible God says that if we agree with him, he won't even remember what we did. He promises to wipe

171

your slate completely clean, as if those sexual experiences had never happened. Remember God never stops loving you, and it makes him happy to make you like new again!"

"What's the catch?" Megan wanted to know.

"The catch is that you can't have sex again until you're married," Tonya told her. "Right, Jan?"

"But my boyfriend will dump me if I stop having sex with him," Christy cried. "He says he loves me and that if I really love him I'll give it to him."

> *Have you ever had sex with a boy because you were afraid you'd lose him if you didn't?*

"Do you really believe that garbage?" Kim asked.

"Whoa! Let's not get nasty," I interrupted. "Christy, remember when we talked about real love? Does what your boyfriend said sound like real love to you? When a boy says he wants to have sex with you outside of marriage, he's really saying, 'I think enough of you to have sex with you, but not enough to commit myself to be your partner for the rest of my life.'

"Marriage is the highest form of social and sexual honor between two people of the opposite sex. A marriage commitment says, 'I love you enough to risk my whole self with you.' Until a person makes that commitment to you, you can never be sure that his love is the kind of real love we've been talking about."

"But we're too young to get married!" Christy wailed.

"Then you're too young to be having sex," I said.

"I'm just so afraid of being alone, of not having anyone care about me. It didn't seem like too much of a price to pay to have someone hold me for a while." Christy began to cry.

I went over and held her. "I know. We feel so isolated and unlovable that we feel we have to pay a price for any affection we ever get. But that's a lie! You have value, Christy. After all, the creator of the whole universe certainly wouldn't die for a nothing. And anyone so valuable deserves to be loved and to experience sex as it was created to be."

"You don't really expect us not to have sex until we're married, do you? I mean, this isn't the 1940s." Sherry was staring at me in disbelief.

"What *I* expect is not the issue here," I told her. "God wants you to move toward *his* plan for beautiful sexuality. That means no sex until you're married.

"I know how hard that can be. Once you've started, it's awfully hard to stop. For some of you, that's the only way you've expressed intimacy and friendship with guys up until now. But if you want the experience of love and sex the way God planned it, you have to stick by his rules."

■ God's Rules

Why does God make up rules? Certainly not because he wants to make you squirm or just because he wants to prove he's God. God is love, remember? He makes the rules to stop us from hurting ourselves. God's rules are part of his true love for us, and true love gives freedom.

Even if you'd never been abused, casual sex with many partners makes it harder for you to have lifelong, committed intimacy with one person. God doesn't want that struggle for you.

Casual sex with many partners also tends to make sexuality into nothing more than just another game. God doesn't want that for you, either.

Sex before marriage weighs down your physical relationship in a real-love marriage with sexual "ghosts" from the past and sexual comparisons. God doesn't want you weighed down with those burdens.

Promiscuity feeds your shame and often leads to a cycle of setting yourself up for more abusive sexual relationships. And God certainly doesn't want that for you.

■ Real Freedom

> *When you're having sex with someone, are you ever afraid?*

"I'm scared sometimes that I'll get caught, depending on where we are when we're doing it," Sherry admitted.

"Aren't you afraid you'll get pregnant?" Christy asked.

"I always make sure the guy has protection." Sherry looked at Christy as if she were stupid.

"But protection doesn't always work. I'm always afraid I'll end up with a baby," Christy responded.

"I'm afraid my parents will find out," Kim interjected. "My dad would kill me if he found out I was fooling around!"

"Listen to what you're saying. Those are some of the very reasons why God doesn't want us to have sex unless we're married to our partners," I said. "Only in marriage can you have real freedom. If you are bound up in fear, guilt,

174

and shame, you don't have the freedom to experience love and sex together as they should be. You don't have the freedom to give yourself completely to another person or the freedom to respond to that person's feelings and desires."

Can you see why God made rules about sexual activity?

"Do you really believe sex can be that good for people like us?" Sherry asked hopefully.

"Yes, I do," I assured her. "I believe everyone can arrive at a place, within the security of marriage, where sex is a celebration. But remember, we all travel at different speeds. For some of us, sex will be a celebration the first time we make love to our husbands. For others, the first time will be beautiful, but it will continue to grow in beauty and wonder until it becomes a celebration. And for others, the first experience may be nothing spectacular. But as we continue to grow in trust and freedom, we'll find ourselves with more fireworks going off around us than a Fourth of July celebration!"

"Which way was it for you and Norm?" Sherry asked.

"Give her a break, Sherry!" Christy exclaimed. "She doesn't have to tell us about her sex life."

"I just thought—" Sherry started.

"No, you didn't think," Christy interrupted.

"Whoa, enough!" I broke in. "It's O.K. Norm and I aren't married yet. That means we don't have sex."

"You mean you've *never* had sex with Norm?!" Sherry clearly displayed her astonishment.

"That's right. The rules are the same for us as they are for you. If we want sex to be a celebration of love instead of

175

just physical gratification, we have to do it God's way, too,"
I told her.

"But both of you already know about love!" Tonya
insisted.

"And we both know what sex is supposed to be, too. I'm
not sure which of us was more surprised to find that the
other knew. He said I was the first person he'd ever known
who understood."

"I sure wish I could find a boyfriend like Norm," Tonya
said wistfully.

"Yeah, he's pretty special," I admitted, "and I'm really
blessed to have him in my life. But you need to remember
that Norm's around my age, and for years he counseled
drug and alcohol abusers. He's also dealt with more of his
own pain and disappointment just because he's older. So,
you see, it would be unrealistic to expect a teenage guy to
have the wisdom and insight Norm has. That's why I told
you it is important for you to find a therapist or pastoral
counselor or someone professional to work with whenever
you get stuck on something.

"Norm's been wonderfully patient and understanding,
but I really wish I'd worked through my problems with sex
before we began our relationship. That's one of the reasons
I work with teens like you, so that you don't find yourselves
in the place where I found myself when Norm came into
my life."

■ **Getting Ready for Your Great Love**

How do you get ready for your great love? Well, believe it
or not, every step you take in your journey is a step closer
to being ready. When you reach out past the fear and trust
someone with what's happened to you, you're closer. When

you learn what love really is and accept the truth that you're worthy of being loved, you're closer. When you understand what sex is really supposed to be and believe that God wants it to be that wonderful for you, you're closer.

Every time you win a victory over shame, you're closer. Every time you take a block out of your fortress of control, you're closer. Every time you throw out a lie that your abuse has taught you and replace it with freedom—the kind of freedom that allows you to build the right kind of relationships—you're getting closer.

So when God brings someone wonderful and understanding into your life, you'll be ready to receive and give real love, and eventually to be united with your husband in the fantastic celebration that God, in his love, created for the two of you. That's what real love and beautiful sexuality are all about.

Moving Ahead

22

The End of the Story

THE GIRLS IN THE GROUP YOU'VE JUST VISITED WERE AT various stages of their journeys when the school year ended. But their journeys didn't end when our group disbanded for the summer.

I wish I could share with you what happened to all of the teens in this book. But there are too many of them. If we followed all of their journeys, this wouldn't be a book; it would be an encyclopedia!

So let's travel with Teresa, the girl whose cousin Mike abused her, to her safe place.

■ Teresa's Journey

Teresa was hurt very deeply, and her years of anger and hatred had led her into all kinds of trouble at home, at school, and in relationships.

Teresa's parents never associated her behavior problems with sexual abuse, and things were getting really

181

tense at home. Teresa continually mouthed off to her mom, and her mom often lost patience with her. Teresa was also heavily into drugs, alcohol, and sex.

Teresa and I met during the summer to work on the trash in her bag of garbage. She had a hard time believing that God would really forgive her for the things she'd been doing. "Why would a good God die for me?" she'd ask.

Teresa was also having a hard time forgiving her mom for making her go to her grandmother's the summer she was abused. "If she really loved me, she wouldn't have made me go." It took awhile for Teresa to accept that her mom had been raised in that house and thought it was a safe place for her daughter while she worked. She had no idea that Mike was molesting Teresa. But there did come a time when Teresa could tell her mom, "I love you."

That summer, Teresa worked through a lot of her hatred for Mike. She decided she needed to confront him before she could move on in her healing. But as the time of the meeting approached, Teresa became more and more agitated. The day before she was to talk to Mike, she got drunk and drove her car off the road.

When Teresa and Mike talked, Mike accepted the responsibility for his actions. He even admitted that when he saw Teresa getting in trouble with boys, he knew it was his fault. He said he would do anything she wanted him to do if it would help her get better. That was what Teresa needed to hear. When he was ready to leave, Teresa hugged him and told him she didn't hate him anymore.

After that, Teresa sat down with me and her parents and wrote out a contract for acceptable behavior and expectations for the whole family. Shortly after the contract was signed, Teresa wrote me the following letter:

Dear Jan,

On the first day of the presentation, I'm not sure
how I felt. I think it was a combination of feelings.
I was scared because I knew all those people in the
group would know I was abused. I was also
hesitant because I thought you were gonna be like
all the other shrinks I'd been to. But after I met
you the first time, I got a new feeling: hope. Then
at the first meeting I was nervous when you
started talking about God. But I was also comfortable because I knew I wasn't alone with my
problems. Since then I think I've really come a long
way. I've given up a lot of things. Drugs—which
were becoming a day-to-day thing. Sex—which was
at least an every-other-day thing. Friends—that I
thought would be there forever. And alcohol—
which wasn't so frequent, but I had a good time
when I did it.

Now I realize that I've gained a lot, too. Aside
from dumb rules, I've gained real love from my
parents, and my relationship with Peter is finally
beginning to move forward. I've also gained a great
friend. But greatest of all, I've come at least to understand Jesus Christ.

Now I have a bunch of feelings like pressure,
depression, happiness, excitement and, weirdest of
all—being reborn.

> Thanks,
> Teresa

Then the bottom fell out!

When Teresa went back to school that fall, she told everyone she was different—"No more slut!" But her old friends just laughed at her and offered her a joint.

Teresa's teachers had come to expect confrontation from her and weren't able to see or appreciate the small concessions to authority that were such a struggle for Teresa to make. One day she became so frustrated that she cursed in the classroom. A conference between Teresa, the assistant principal, and me ended hotly. He was exhausted by students who didn't accept authority.

Teresa was suspended for three days. I talked to her the next day, and she assured me that she wasn't upset anymore and that everything was just fine. But the next time one of her friends offered her a joint, she took it.

Teresa will tell you now that she was angry at God because she had started to do drugs again. She felt as if she couldn't talk to him anymore because she wasn't good anymore.

Then Teresa ran away from home. Her parents and I tracked her down. I called and told her that if she wasn't on her way home in an hour, her parents would call the police and have her picked up and have the man she was with arrested for contributing to the delinquency of a minor. She cursed at me. I told her I loved her.

She came home. We added rules to the contract. She broke them again and refused to comply with the penalties.

For the next few months Teresa did everything she could think of to show how really bad she was. Her behavior at home became intolerable. Then one weekend when her father had to be out of town, she hit her mother and ran away again.

This time she was harder to find. Even her boyfriend Peter, who really cared about her, didn't know how to find her. Finally I tracked her down; but when I got to where she was staying, she was out with the girl she was living with and some boys.

That evening I asked my church to pray for Teresa. I explained how she had tried to stand up as a new person at school, but how her friends had laughed and how the "good" kids wouldn't accept her. I told them I was afraid she was going to kill herself—with drugs, in a car, some way—because she felt she didn't deserve to live.

That night thirteen teens left church with me to go back to the place where Teresa was staying. They wanted to tell her they'd be her friends. We waited for her. She came home high, but she was coherent enough to realize that those kids had waited because they really did care about what happened to her.

I took her to my house. Over the phone, her parents and I agreed that Teresa should be placed in a lock-up program for teens with drug-abuse problems. Teresa was furious.

"Jan, please don't do this to me! Talk to Daddy. Don't let them lock me up!" she begged.

"I can't do that, Teresa." I didn't expect her to understand, but I tried to explain. "We love you too much not to do this. You'll kill yourself if you keep on like you are, and you know it."

"I don't care," she cried. "I don't want to be locked up."

"You might not care, but we do," I told her.

She didn't ask again.

After only two days, Teresa escaped from the adolescent care unit with another girl and two boys. They drank and had sex together. When they finally came back to the hospital, the director refused to let them reenter the program.

Teresa's parents placed her in a private adolescent drug lock-up program in a city about fifty miles away. The counselors there realized that Teresa's drug abuse was a symptom of a larger problem—her childhood sexual abuse.

Fifteen weeks later, Teresa had a happy "graduation" from lock-up, but she was afraid to leave. She knew her old friends would be waiting. She wasn't sure she was strong enough to keep them out of her life, and she knew she would end up dead if she didn't.

But this time was different. Teresa had the strength to hold on to her family's love and to God's love. She went back to school and graduated with her class. Peter had waited for her, and they were married that summer.

Recently I had a wonderful visit with Teresa. She's now a healthy, happy, pregnant wife.

"Do you ever wonder where you would be now if you hadn't gotten in the group?" I asked her as we sat in the swing behind her parents' home.

"Oh, I know exactly where I'd be," she replied. "I'd be dead."

We were both silent for a few moments, then she smiled. "You know, I never would have thought that God could have taken the mess my life was and worked it out for good for so many people," she said.

"Oh, I would have!" I told her. "That's God's favorite job, and he's really good at it!"

From the time I first met Teresa to the time when she got a firm grasp on her life was a long haul, one full of struggle and setbacks. And she knows there will be events in her future that will probably trigger an old feeling or an old fear. But Teresa has found her safe place, a place lighted by the truth where she can safely deal with those feelings and work through those fears.

■ A Safe Place

Teresa reached her safe place. And that's what I want for you. As you've seen, it won't be an easy journey, but you can make it!

As I sit here tonight in front of my computer writing the final pages of this book, I know I may not have the blessing of getting to know you personally. I wish I could walk with you and wipe away your tears as you cry out your pain and anger and bitterness. I wish I could look into your eyes and make you understand how important and valuable and beautiful and lovable you are.

I wish I could share your joy as you gain the freedom to be all you are created to be, the freedom to receive and to give true love, the freedom to experience the beautiful celebration of love.

But I can't. So my prayer for you is that what we've shared in this book will give you hope and that your hope will give you the courage to begin your own journey.

I've asked God to let the truth about your abuse and your worth in his eyes shed new light on the experiences of your past. I've asked him to help you find a safe place in that light as you journey through the mountains and valleys in your life—a place away from the swirling confusion of whirlpools that can suck you down, a path through the thick undergrowth of lies, a secure foothold to keep you from falling at the rough places.

I've asked God to give each of you so much of his real love that it will flow through you into all your relationships. And I've asked God to provide each of you who wishes to

187

marry with someone who can share the celebration of love with you.

As you make your journey, my biggest hope for you is that you'll discover God, the One who is *always* there, the One who always understands, who always loves you unconditionally, no matter what.

Just for You

My reason for writing this book is to give you hope—hope that there is a way through the effects of sexual abuse . . . hope that you can get beyond your abuse to a safe place where you can continue to grow in truth and love for the rest of your life. I hope that's what this book has done—given you enough hope and courage to make the decision to start on your own journey. If it has, I want to give you some suggestions on how to get started.

Find a trusted adult who can help you locate a pastoral counselor or therapist to help you sort out the garbage. And ask your counselor to find a support group you can join so you can experience the understanding and acceptance of others like yourself as you travel.

Keep this book tucked away somewhere so that when you feel alone, overwhelmed by the length of your journey, or when it seems like you're slipping back four steps for every one you take forward, you can pull it out and read the chapters that deal with the areas you're struggling with. Read about Teresa and the struggles she had before she found her safe place. Read about how much God loves you—and about the wonder of true love and sex that he wants you to experience.

Keep telling yourself the truth about your abuse and the way your abuse has caused you to act. Remember: *All the guilt and shame belongs always and only to your abuser—never to you!*

If you need help, write to:

Tree of Rest, Inc.
P.O. Box 6321
Virginia Beach, VA 23456

or call toll-free:

1-800-782-9834

Tree of Rest, Inc.

Tree of Rest, Inc. is a non-profit corporation that provides assembly presentations, education, and support training in the field of sexual abuse to public schools, community organizations, counseling centers, police departments, young people's groups, and churches.

Tree of Rest was founded by Jan Morrison in 1986. Beginning as a part-time endeavor, it grew dramatically in response to the demand for the help it offers sexually abused teens.

Prior to the organization's conception, Jan's position as a consultant to 80 high schools in North Carolina placed her in direct contact with counselors, teachers, administrators, and students. One teacher, knowing of Jan's personal experience with sexual abuse, asked Jan to speak to her class. The impact of the presentation was immediately evident.

Throughout the school, students were discussing the program. Other teachers requested that Jan speak to their classes. Counselors began to discuss and recommend her presentation at district and regional meetings. Soon she was speaking at student assemblies in the area.

Following the presentations, students would often approach Jan and tell her of their own experiences, experiences that they were either afraid or ashamed to discuss before hearing her speak. The pain she saw in these young people convinced her of the need to develop an extensive program to help students deal with the effects of sexual abuse. She was concerned that teens be helped *before* leaving school, before they became entrapped in life-styles that would perpetuate both their own abuse and the abuse of future generations.

One of Jan's first activities was to enlist the aid of a team of experts: a counselor recognized by the court system as an expert in the field of child sexual abuse, a high-school administrator, an attorney, a pastor, and several high-school counselors and teachers. Together, they created the unique programs that are now offered by Tree of Rest.

The success of the organization brought Jan invitations to speak on national radio and television broadcasts. Soon the overwhelming number of requests for the program resulted in Jan's decision to devote herself full-time to the work of Tree of Rest.

In January 1989, Tree of Rest, Inc. relocated in the Chicago metropolitan area in order to help a greater number of young people in a concentrated geographic area.

■ High-School Program

The Tree of Rest program for high schools has two main emphases: 1) educating individuals about sexual abuse and 2) providing assistance for students who were victims, through both direct intervention by Tree of Rest and training of support people within the school system and community. The structure includes three phases: *set-up, presentation,* and *follow-up.*

Phase One: Set-up

The set-up phase begins with contacting members of various organizations and professional services within the community. School personnel (counselors, teachers, and principals) are educated about sexual abuse.

Participants not only learn the causes and effects of sexual abuse but also how to recognize behavioral, physical, and familial indicators of abuse and how to reach out effectively in true understanding to the teenager who has been sexually abused.

Tree of Rest also assists school administrators in formatting procedures for handling reports of sexual abuse made to, or about, school personnel. Ethical and legal issues are considered in framing policies.

While phase one deals with those who will assist and support, phases two and three focus on direct help for the victim.

Phase Two: Presentation

Dealing with the Effects of Sexual Abuse BEFORE You Enter the Real World is a school assembly presentation in which Jan Morrison shares her dynamic life story and extends the opportunity for students to share their thoughts, experiences, and concerns privately with her. (Of those who have attended school assemblies, approximately 10 percent have come in for one-to-one conversations with Jan.)

Phase Three: Follow-up

In this phase, Tree of Rest, Inc. will either train school personnel or arrange for local counselors to lead victim support groups.

Tree of Rest's program is extensive—it does not consist of only one assembly or a one-time session. The program offers continuing consultation for school personnel involved in administering programs or helping students. Follow-up and care continue to all those who need and desire it.

■ Programs for Churches

Tree of Rest offers four Christian programs for churches.

His Healing Through His Body: Christ's Answer for Those Affected by Sexual Abuse

This comprehensive program has as its goal to minister God's healing to all those effected by the sin of sexual abuse.

Workers can be trained to facilitate groups that provide a safe place for victims and families to receive the true healing of God.

"Alongside Teams" can be trained to: (1) assist victims and their families with their involvement with the legal and judicial systems (2) work with perpetrators to assure that the light of God's truth is shed on any program into which they may be adjudicated, as well as to hold him/her accountable for their personal relationship with God and (3) help spouses of perpetrators work through their responses to the discovery that they are married to an abuser.

In addition, since it would be almost impossible for a church to offer programs covering all potential needs of a family struggling through the legal and/or healing issues resulting from sexual abuse, the networking arm of the program interfaces with community agencies and organizations as well as the law enforcement and judicial systems to direct victims and families to services such as financial assistance, child care, food pantries, etc. not provided by the church.

A person or persons chosen by the church will be trained to administer the overall sexual abuse program, train incoming workers, and establish the network system for the church.

In Safe Hands

A three-day retreat for victims and survivors of sexual abuse, the objective of this program is to prepare participants to begin their healing.

Learning the truth of how God views sexual abuse and the unconditional love He has for victims, plus being bathed in prayer and ministered to in love by retreat workers, allows participants to remove the armor with which they have sought to protect themselves and replace it with the armor of God. Thus protected they are ready to take back the ground the enemy has gained in their lives—through lies learned through abuse about who God is, who they are to Him, and what that means for them.

Safe Church

This sweeping strategy was designed to protect (1) infants, children, and teens from abuse, (2) Christian workers from false accusations and (3) the church from both criminal and civil liability.

Screening helps to bar perpetrators from infiltrating infant, child, and teen programs. Education of staff and volunteers alerts workers to behavior that could be misinterpreted, as well as equipping them to recognize techniques and tactics utilized by perpetrators.

Securing programs sponsored by the church (whether or not they take place on church property) with strictly enforced policies, and securing facilities by certain structural requirements protects both children and workers because it lessens the opportunity for either actual abuse or unfounded accusation.

Implementing these procedures and policies not only provides protection for children and workers but will help annul any charges of criminal or civil negligence on the part of the church, should abuse occur.

Healing the Church of Sexual Abuse

Most pastors and church leaders confronted with an instance of sexual abuse perpetrated by a staff member or volunteer recognize that measures taken with the usual cases of moral failure simply do not apply. They are face to face with a crisis that nothing in their educational background or their personal experience has prepared them to deal with.

Since each situation is different, the procedures and time frames for this program will vary. However, it can lay out for all the parties involved what to expect, focusing first on the church, then the victim and his/her family, the perpetrator and his/her family, and others directly involved or affected.

Interaction with law enforcement and the judicial system by Tree of Rest personnel offers a good impression of not only the church's willingness but its ability to respond correctly. These workers have extensive experience both in working with the system, with making sound evaluations, and where necessary, putting together programs approved by the legal/judicial system.

The counsel and assistance provided by Tree of Rest both during the critical first few hours and days following discovery as well as the strategic approach to long-term situations and issues can mean the difference between a devastated, split congregation and a united body.

Consultation and referral services are available from Tree of Rest, Inc. at any time. Intercessory prayer for churches involved with the program is ongoing.

For more information write

Tree of Rest, Inc.
P.O. Box 6321
Virginia Beach, VA 23456

or call:
1-804-721-2095

Dear Parents,

1988 was a nightmare for my family. But our seventeen-year-old daughter had been living with nightmares of her own since the summer she turned eight. That summer, she was sexually abused by her fifteen-year-old second cousin. The abuse took place not only once but throughout the summer. Both were staying with their grandparents while my husband and I worked.

To keep her from telling what was happening to her, our daughter was threatened with harm to her grandparents and her younger sister. Out of fear she kept the truth inside until her dating years began. Her ideas of love were destroyed. She blamed us for not protecting her.

When we heard what had happened, we felt like killing her abuser. Our daughter asked us to leave it alone, to let it die. She felt that telling us would be enough to help her forget. We were afraid to take any steps that might bring it all back. We hoped she would be able to forget, but things only got worse.

Before the school year ended for the summer, she joined a sex-abuse support group started by Jan Morrison of Tree of Rest. In that group she was able to discuss all the tragic things that she was too embarrassed to share with us. It helped her feel better about herself to discuss her experience with others who had gone through the same thing.

At first things seemed to be better. Then our daughter began breaking curfews and being violently abusive of us. We tried to give her things to show her that she was somebody—a car, new clothes, etc. But we didn't realize how much she hated herself.

She wanted to be punished, and she tried us in every possible way. There were countless nights when she didn't come home until the early morning hours. We'd search for her, call the hospitals to see if she'd been in an accident, and even call the police to see if she had been arrested. She'd come home and treat us like dirt, offering no explanations of where she had been. She even struck her father, whom she loved more than anyone in the world.

Jan seemed to be the only person she didn't try to lie to. She knew that Jan had been there and knew all the tricks.

Our daughter's poor opinion of herself led her to drugs and alcohol. She totalled her car, receiving internal injuries. She continued to do drugs. And we were unaware that she even had the problem.

One weekend when her father was away on business, she attacked me. Although my husband had encouraged me to call the police if I had problems, can you imagine calling the police about your own child? The police talked with her. She ended up leaving home. That Sunday night, we called Jan. She found our daughter, and the next morning Jan and my husband took our daughter to a rehab center and had her tested for drugs. She was admitted immediately.

Now our daughter is growing better every day in every way—family, love, trust, self-respect. She has come a very long way.

Kids are afraid to tell their parents because they think their parents won't love them as much if they know they've been abused. In fact, kids sometimes blame themselves more than anyone else.

Somebody has to be there for these kids. And that's why Jan has written this book—to show teenagers like our daughter that there is hope for them if they will seek help for their problems.

I think all teenagers should read this book. If they've been abused, they'll be able to see that there is a way through their problems. If they haven't, it will help them understand what's going on inside their friends who have been abused. And the right kind of support from friends can make all the difference in the world.

Our family knows it's not easy to deal with abuse, but we shudder to think what could have happened to our daughter if she hadn't gotten help.

Teresa's mom

Endorsements

I have had the pleasure of working with Jan on the formulation and presentation of two seminars on the recognition, treatment, and prevention of child sexual abuse in North Carolina. I consider her to be a dedicated, talented, and energetic person who gives herself wholeheartedly to any project she begins.
—**David B. Peters,** Author of *A Betrayal of Innocence,* and Minister of Counseling, Chapel in the Pines

Jan Morrison's ministry will challenge any church or lay group to a more compassionate outreach to hurting people. She has discovered and demonstrates Christ's ability to heal the wounded spirit. God has given her a unique sense of humor, and the fact that she has this after all the pain she has suffered speaks volumes for the power of the Gospel.
—**Larry L. Patton,** General Manager, Trinity Broadcasting Network, Inc., Greensboro, North Carolina and Atlanta, Georgia

I have known Jan Morrison since 1986. During that time I have found her to be a dedicated Christian who has chosen to serve the Lord in a unique ministry to young persons who are victims of sexual abuse. All who work with her believe in what she does. She is reliable and has real integrity.
—**William P. Wilson,** Professor Emeritus of Psychiatry, Duke University

During the time Jan Morrison was in Macon County to hold lectures on the subject of child sex abuse, she assisted me with complaints which came to light. As an investigator, I found her ability to develop a good rapport with the adults and children involved to be vastly important.
—**Gene Ledford,** Director of Juvenile Services, Macon County Sheriff's Department

Teenagers need to know about, understand, and explore this problem of child sexual abuse. It is only through honest and open exploration that we can bring to light potential problems in this area of child sexual abuse. Many students at Western High School have been helped through Jan's follow-up conferences and countless others have given serious consideration to this problem as a result of Jan's presentation. For this, I will be eternally grateful.
—**Carl S. Herman,** Principal, Western Alamance High School

From the very beginning of her ministry to us, Jan was hard-working and well-focused. All of her efforts are based upon Scripture and are prayer-powered. Whether Jan was addressing our congregation as a whole or any one individual involved in the process, she was clearly competent. She

is very strategic in her approach, capable of being both sensitive and straightforward. Without reservation or hesitation, I heartily recommend Jan Morrison's ministry.
—**David L. Clark,** Pastor, Central Christian Church, Beloit, Wisconsin

When our church discovered an ongoing case of molestation, the Lord graciously directed our pathway to Jan Morrison and the Tree of Rest ministry. Her expertise and compassion gave us all a sense of great relief and trust. Jan simply moved in, "set up shop," and decisively began to lay out for all the parties involved what to expect. She focused first on the victim and his family, confronted the perpetrator, developed a plan with the full knowledge of the District Attorney, and trained the entire church body concerning sexual abuse. I recommend the ministry of Jan to you without reservation.
Ron J. Bontrager, Pastor, Lakewood Assembly of God, Indianapolis, Indiana